The Attributes Of Joseph

The Attributes of Joseph

Ancient Principles for Modern Success

By
Rusty Davis

E-BookTime, LLC
Montgomery, Alabama

The Attributes of Joseph
Ancient Principles for Modern Success

ISBN: 978-1-60862-520-8

First Edition
Published September 2013
E-BookTime, LLC
6598 Pumpkin Road
Montgomery, AL 36108
www.e-booktime.com

Acknowledgements

I am so thankful for the many wonderful people God has brought into my life over the years. I am the person I am because God has molded me through relationships with incredible people. This is an opportunity to thank some of them.

Obviously, I first thank God for his never-ending grace and mercy. He has protected, provided, and guided me through these first fifty years. Each and every day I appreciate more and more the love that he feels for his children.

Thanks to my incredible wife, Sherri, and daughter, Shayla. I am truly the luckiest man alive to have such a wonderful wife and daughter. Thank you for your love, encouragement, and support! Life has been made much richer because of my girls. Also, many thanks to Lucky, Donna, Linda, Scott, Jim and Julie for allowing me to be a part of your family.

I am forever grateful for the wonderful memories of my dad who provided and influenced me for 37 years. I miss him daily and miss him dearly. We will meet again someday, and I will thank him again. Thanks to my mother who continues to love and support her sons like no other. You have been a constant through all these years, never ceasing to sacrifice for me. My wonderful brother, Randy, who has been the consummate big brother, thanks for having my back!

I could never thank all of the wonderful people I have worked with over the years. These associates, mentors, and friends have shaped the person I am, and I thank them all!

Preface

Why do success, fulfillment, and purpose in life seem to be so illusive? Why do Americans, despite an enormous advantage over the vast majority of people throughout the world, seem to be so disillusioned and unsatisfied? Despite incredible and incomparable advantages and opportunity, so many Americans seem to live average, mundane, if not disappointing, lives. Despite the abundant resources at our disposal, so many Americans seem to be frustrated. So many seem to be cynical toward the future and almost resigned to a subpar and uneventful existence. Why do so many Americans seem to chase a shadow they never can catch?

Americans spend billions of dollars each year on self-improvement and motivational books. We visit sweat lodges and hire personal coaches in an effort to improve our odds of success. We constantly seek new trends and fads to achieve success and fulfillment. But yet, so few of us seem to truly achieve total success, complete fulfillment, and rewarding purpose in life. It seems so many of us languish in average jobs, produce average results, and live through average experiences as we navigate through an unspectacular existence. Those grandiose dreams we dreamed when we were younger seem to get pummeled and beaten by a vicious reality. Too often our lofty desires are pushed to the back of our imagination as real life chokes the hope from us. Ambitions and visions of dreams coming true are crushed and thrown to the four winds. Eventually, after being beaten down by disappointment after crushing disappointment, we simply give up on our spectacular dreams and desires. Eventually, we simply hope to make it to retirement, fizzle out the last few years of our life, and die.

Some do experience vocational and material success while sacrificing the important relationships in their lives. Some experience success, but they often lack fulfillment and seek it through other destructive channels like alcohol, drugs, and other deadly vices. Others may experience fulfillment but not consider themselves successful. Others possess clarity regarding their purpose in life, but lack success and fulfillment. Others experience great relationships in their lives, but seem to miss out on success. It seems truly difficult to score the "hat-trick," or achieve true success, fulfillment, and purpose.

I think somewhere along the way, our perception of success, fulfillment, and purpose has been skewed. This is due in large part to the commercialized culture we live in. We have been brainwashed into believing that true success can only be achieved through substantial accomplishments, accumulation of wealth, and obtaining positions of prestige and power. We think that fulfillment can only be obtained through the acquisition and compilation of more assets. Our only purpose seems to be to make more money, acquire more wealth, compare ourselves to others more, and consume more.

This book examines the well-vetted life of Joseph, the favorite son of Jacob, and how he achieved incredible success, fulfillment, and purpose. Those who are familiar with the Bible know the story well. We have heard about the brothers betraying him, his coat of many colors, and how Joseph possessed the ability to interpret dreams. This book digs deeper into the traits and attributes that Joseph practiced. Hopefully we can learn how to integrate these attributes into our lives to live much more fulfilling and successful lives.

Yes, Joseph did accomplish and accumulate material wealth. But the accumulation of wealth or obtaining a prestigious, powerful position alone does not necessarily guarantee success, fulfillment, and purpose. Success, fulfillment, and purpose are intertwined, or comingled; they go hand in hand. To experience life at its fullest, we need to experience success in our given space or place and sense fulfillment and satisfaction from our work, relationships, and accomplishments. Finally, while experiencing success and fulfillment, our sense of purpose is recognized. It is then that life is enriching.

I am not suggesting that only Christians or believers can experience success, fulfillment, and a sense of purpose in life. There are certainly innumerable case studies of people who have experienced success without a faith or "Christian" experience. What I am suggesting is that God designed a blue print for total success, and it does include him, his presence in our lives, and it includes us as humans working in harmony with him. So, this book is not just for Christians seeking success. But to experience the level of success and fulfillment that Joseph experienced, I do truly believe it must include a real relationship with God. Experiencing and walking with God certainly makes integrating the attributes into your life easier, although one can adhere to these attributes without a faith experience.

Additionally, please do not shut this down if you are not a Christian. I would encourage you to continue reading. There is so much to learn from Joseph's responses to the challenges he experienced in life. These lessons are not exclusive only to Christians. The experiences, emotions, and challenges Joseph faced are the same challenges that every human of every race and every belief faces. Every human, regardless of beliefs or un-beliefs, can learn how to respond positively to negative obstacles if we observe Joseph's behavior.

In our modern era, we think of legendary business moguls like Steve Jobs, Bill Gates, Warren Buffet, and Mark Zuckerburg as huge successes. Yes, they have certainly achieved monumental material success and changed the way our world lives. But only they could say whether they have obtained fulfillment and purpose.

There was an inside joke in our family for many years. My wife and I would plan a vacation to somewhere we had never been. Our daughter, very young at the time, could hardly contain her excitement thinking about these places we were going. She always visualized in her mind what these places would be like. Inevitably, almost every time we finally arrived at the destination, she would seem disappointed. She would often say, "It's just not what I thought it would be." I think that is how we are with success. We think that accomplishing a goal, reaching a mile-stone, or passing a significant marker will bring us that sense of satisfaction we seek. When in all actuality, just achieving a goal, or obtaining a position, or buying a larger house, will not provide us the gratification we seek. Complete success and fulfillment comes through accomplishments, contentment, and fulfilling relationships.

Goals, accomplishments, promotions, prestige, and the accumulation of material wealth can be part of the experience on our path to true success and fulfillment, but they cannot, alone, fulfill our lives or provide us the sense of satisfaction we truly desire. Joseph obviously wanted to succeed, but he also wanted to be fulfilled, and he wanted to live out his purpose in life. As we explore these attributes he practiced, we will see that by aligning success, fulfillment, and purpose, we can truly achieve that pinnacle of happiness that Joseph experienced. A combination of these three pursuits can bring us the ultimate sense of fulfillment.

Experiencing true success is about finding your niche, discovering what you are good at, and finding what you are passionate about doing and doing it for a living. Fulfillment comes from being content with your career, your personal life, your relationships, and being happy in your current environment. You may be working toward more lofty goals, but you are content and happy with your current situation. A sense of purpose means you understand your position, your strengths, and your optimum zone for effectiveness in every aspect of your life. Your purpose and my purpose are to touch those in our circles of influence in a positive way. Our purpose is to help, encourage, and serve mankind. Joseph had all of these things. Joseph had his priorities in order. We may experience the same fulfillment and purpose that Joseph experienced, but we may not experience the same material success.

Many achieve tremendous financial success and amass fortunes. But sadly, they often discover that they are hollow, empty, and discontent. How many rich, famous celebrities have committed suicide over the decades? How many politicians, athletes, and executives have fallen from their lofty positions due to reckless and immoral decisions or misconduct? I truly think it is because somewhere along the way, they lost touch or focus with the attributes that Joseph integrated into his life.

Of all the inspirational stories in the Old Testament of the Bible, I have always been especially fascinated with the life of

Joseph, son of Jacob and Rachel. One of twelve brothers, he is the obvious favorite of his father. Out of jealousy and resentment, his brothers sell him to slave traders who sell him to an Egyptian military leader. Joseph earns favor with the leader and is placed in charge of his household. Then, just when he seems to be hitting his stride, he is falsely accused of attacking his master's wife and sent to prison to languish indefinitely. There, he once again gains favor with the head of the prison guard and is given much authority within the prison. Later, while in prison, he interprets two dreams, one for the King's baker, and the other for the King's wine taster. The dreams come to pass as Joseph predicted, and Joseph asks the baker to tell Pharaoh about him and his ability to interpret dreams when he returns to Pharaoh's service, but the baker forgets. Joseph is in prison two more years when Pharaoh has a couple of dreams that no one can interpret. The baker finally remembers Joseph and tells Pharaoh about his ability to interpret dreams. Joseph is summoned to interpret Pharaoh's dreams, and he predicts with salient and crystal clear accuracy the seven years of plenty followed by seven years of severe famine. Pharaoh is so impressed with Joseph that he places him second in command only to the King.

Joseph plans out the strategy for the next fourteen years. Egypt stores up grain during the years of plenty, and when the famine strikes, the people of Egypt have food. The famine is so severe it impacts the entire region of the world. Not only did Joseph's actions save the Egyptians from starvation, but due to his vision, wisdom, and guidance from God, he provides food to the surrounding countries. Eventually, Joseph is reconnected with his brothers and father in a tearful reunion.

Joseph marries, has children, and watches his people integrate into Egyptian society and culture. Joseph's sons are blessed by Jacob before he dies, and Joseph, after a successful, fulfilling, and purpose-driven life, passes away when he is one hundred and ten years old. Joseph's faithfulness, obedience, and trust in God leads him to a very rewarding life while laying the groundwork for the Exodus out of Egypt a few hundred years later under the leadership of Moses.

Despite enormous diversions, setbacks, and detours, Joseph never lost faith in God. He never compromised his principles and continued to work hard with a precision, laser-like focus. He possessed a wide array of communication skills, interpersonal skills, and strategic skills that we all can learn and integrate into our lives. In the end, Joseph forgave his family for the atrocities committed against him and recognized that all of these events were orchestrated by God to place him where he needed to be. If anyone could have been bitter about their circumstances in life, it could have been Joseph. While I am sure he experienced discouragement, frustration, and bewilderment regarding his path in life, as anyone would, there is no indication that Joseph ever doubted God or turned his back on him.

Joseph's Early Years

The writer of Genesis covers a considerable amount of time in the story of Joseph. The story is told at a "forty thousand foot view" or from a "macro" viewpoint. While covering a vast period of time, the author does not go into great detail about the specific responses, feelings, habits, traits, and insights into Joseph's daily life. Nonetheless, there are numerous clues, glimpses, and hints to the attributes that Joseph lived by that contributed to the ultimate success in his life. Let's explore this amazing life of Joseph, different from any other character in scripture, and see if we can learn from his life.

Some might argue that Joseph was pre-destined by God to achieve what he achieved, and thus nothing could have derailed his ultimate destiny. Since God had great things in store for Joseph, he simply had to show up. I disagree. I think God has much success and potential planned for everyone, however, he does his part, and we are expected to do our part to see great accomplishments come to pass. God may indeed have great things planned for us, but we have to apply ourselves and put forth the effort to see them happen. God does not simply wave a wand and give us what he wants us to achieve.

Every human being possesses tremendous potential. Some of us are born into better circumstances and environments that make success much easier to achieve. Conditions like a well-rounded family life, adequate financial resources, and a great support system can certainly grease the tracks for one to achieve success.

However, I have seen people rise from the unlikeliest circumstances and achieve much. I have seen people overcome tremendous obstacles and achieve great success. As a famous philosopher once said, "All men have the same nature. It is their individual habits that differentiate them." Likewise, I have seen many who had tremendous resources squander the opportunities presented to them.

God gives each of us the potential for success. However, so many times, sometimes through faults of our own and sometimes due to circumstances of which we have no control, our potential is derailed, and we are prevented from achieving what God had designed for us.

Yes, I think Joseph possessed much potential. He recognized his potential and accepted his destiny, and practiced behaviors that assured him of success, fulfillment, and purpose. If we are lucky, we will realize we have tremendous potential. Every human being is a unique creation with unique perceptions, expressions of communications, strengths, and gifts. There are immeasurable opportunities to touch and reach others in need. Like all of us, Joseph encountered many distractions, discouragements, and obstacles along the way that could have easily diverted his quest for success, but he practiced and engrained into his behavior and attitudes certain attributes that assured him of ultimate success, fulfillment, and purpose.

Though Genesis does not go into great detail about Joseph's formative years, one could conclude that Joseph was taught sound, "faith-based" principles by his parents. After all, his father was Jacob, his grandfather was Isaac, and his great grandfather was Abraham. He did come from a rich lineage of early Jewish faith founders, also known as the "Patriarchs," but he also came from an obviously dysfunctional family with many flaws and shortcomings.

It is reasonable to assume that Joseph was trained by his parents at an early age to develop a meaningful prayer relationship with God and to seek God's guidance, wisdom, and insight in every facet of his life. Likely, he observed Jacob and Rachel practicing daily routines consistent with mature believers. There was no written scripture in Joseph's time as we know it today, so I can only presume that Jacob shared the stories of his fathers and grandfathers orally with his children. Interestingly, Joseph is the only significant character in the Old Testament where no real failure is reported.

While writing an essay for a college Bible class a few years ago, I began to take a hard look at the successes Joseph experienced in his life. I began to identify attributes that really made him a model for those of us seeking success, fulfillment, and purpose in life. I truly think we can experience maximum success in our lives if we will study these attributes. By meditating on these ancient attributes practiced by Joseph, I sincerely believe we can lead more successful, meaningful lives at work, in our relationships with our families, and most importantly, in our relationship with God. Dwell on these attributes of Joseph, make a focused, concerted effort on each of them, pray that God will assist you in developing and obtaining these attributes, and let God help you reach your full potential.

You will notice, and I emphasize throughout the book, that these attributes are intertwined; in other words, they work hand in hand, and one builds on the other. For example, achieving contentment, or maintaining character and integrity, may prove difficult without possessing spiritual maturity. All of the attributes truly complement each other. Once again, I am not saying that there are not successful people in the world who do not practice these attributes; there certainly are. However, the point of this book is to help you achieve well-rounded, complete success. I do think these attributes are most effective for those hoping to build on their faith, have a significant positive impact on others on their given circle of influence, and to ultimately advance the kingdom of God.

Joseph possessed the same propensity to fail as anyone else. However, he chose not to fail. He knew this would be a weak reflection of his faith in God. He developed an invincible resolve to accomplish what needed to be accomplished. Surely Joseph had times of doubt and discouragement as we all do. But Joseph knew to let those doubts glance off of him and to keep a laser-like focus on the tasks at hand.

A Glimpse of Destiny

Joseph had visions when he was young. In these visions, he saw himself ruling over his brothers someday. He did not know how these visions would come to pass. I am sure that when he was being hauled to Egypt by slave traders after being betrayed by his brothers, he wondered if these visions were a mistake, a destiny that would not be fulfilled. However, Joseph kept living the life he knew he was supposed to live and left the fulfillment of his destiny up to God. Joseph knew all along that he was destined for greatness. Thus, he did not question the detours along the way, nor did he question how it happened. By practicing the attributes, he trusted his destiny was in God's hands.

Granted, Joseph had the visions about him ruling over his brothers, but he was not sure of the context of this vision. You might think that he had the advantage of true revelation of his destiny, thus he never wavered in his faith that it would come to pass. While we may not possess Joseph's ability to interpret dreams, I think we all see hints of our destiny at times. Surely you have sensed a feeling of inspiration regarding an idea, or a business, or a cause. Surely you envisioned the fulfillment of a goal or a desire. I think this sense of intuitiveness or vision is God's way of showing us our potential destiny. We cannot let the disappointments, failures, setbacks, and trials in our lives dull or blur our vision of our destiny.

Joseph was chosen as an instrument in God's plan because God knew he had the potential, the faithfulness, the tenacity, and the determination to carry out his plan. No one else was chosen for Joseph's mission. You have been chosen for your particular mission. I have been chosen for my particular mission. No one else has been chosen to be where you are right now. You are who you are, where you are, wherever that may be, through pure divine intervention. That alone should give you a sense of empowerment. God knows your potential, and he has a plan in your life. That is an overwhelming concept if you dwell on it. What great accomplishments may await us if we adapt these attributes into our lives and trust God to lead us on our journey?

Who Am I?

I am just a normal, ordinary American man. I long for success, security, and happiness for my family and myself, much like anyone else. I have experienced much success in my life, but I have certainly fallen short of the potential God has granted me. I believe God has great things planned out for us if we are receptive to his guidance. I believe God can lead us through very profound and effective lives if we will allow him and not shackle him. If God is truly the center of our existence, I believe great things can occur. Joseph realized this and accepted that God was leading his life, even when his path seemed uncertain.

This book is a challenge to myself and hopefully will challenge you to ponder and evaluate your life. I hope this book will challenge you to dig deep inside yourself and determine if you possess and practice each of these attributes. If not, I am hopeful you will work at improving the areas of weakness. I hope to achieve the same. I hope this book will help you harness and leverage the strengths you possess and choke out the weaknesses that hinder and obstruct your path to a complete life. Joseph's life is an incredible and salient portal into the limitless potential God wants to execute through us. I truly believe this record of Joseph's life was written to remind you and me that through God everything is possible.

I know from my own experiences, and from observing the experiences of others, that we are often our own biggest obstacle. Our finite minds, not God's infinite mind, hold us back from achieving so much in life. Like the drag on a parachute induced by the air, our limited capacity to understand and to recognize the omnipotent power of God slows our stride toward success. We construct constraints on our own potential. We place limitations on what we think God can do through us. Perhaps we were told when we were young that we did not possess the talent, intelligence, or power to achieve great things. As a result, we stored those destructive opinions into our memory banks, only to replay the destructive loop of criticisms throughout our lives. Hopefully this book will help you realize that you and I are powerful beings with a tremendous force in our lives. If we allow God to use us as he intends, our lives will become very exciting.

I am not an author by trade, nor am I a theologian. I have worked in the private sector in the banking industry and in sales for twenty-five years. I am an astute observer of human behavior and have spent many years evaluating and analyzing traits and practices of highly successful people and others who have not been as successful. I believe firmly that life should be a continuous learning experience and that God wants us, as his children, to constantly strive to be more effective citizens, Christians, parents, leaders, and employees.

I have been a Christian most of my life. There have been times when I have felt close to God, and there have been times when I felt there was a million miles between us. There have been times when I was focused on improving my Christian experience and times when I put it on a shelf. There have been times when I have treated people with compassion and concern and times when I have been rude and selfish. In the end, I would say I am just an ordinary man.

I am just an average, middle-class, working American who has been very blessed with good health and a happy, healthy family. Our family has been extremely blessed, but we have faced our trials like anyone else. However, I would not trade my life for anyone's in the world. With each passing day, I come to realize that I am truly the most blessed man in the world. There are millions of people all over the world and right here in my country that would give everything to have health, a good marriage, a good job, and a decent life like mine.

I have read countless books, magazines, periodicals, etc. regarding self-improvement, motivation, and success. I feel that I constantly need to be re-energized, re-invigorated, and spurred along to achieve my full potential. The study of these attributes is as much for my own advancement and fulfillment as they are for anyone else. I am constantly exploring ways to be more effective, impactful, successful, and fulfilled.

There is nothing mystical or supernatural regarding the Joseph attributes. I did not receive any mysterious revelations from the tombs of the Pharaohs or from the graves of the ancient patriarchs. This is not really a self-help or "discover the secret" motivational book. This book is simply the result of an extensive study and observations of one of the most successful men in ancient history, a man who, despite great adversity, managed to stay focused on his duty to God and accomplished great things materially, spiritually, and relationally, without compromising his principles. There were no shortcuts for Joseph.

There are no earth-shattering revelations in the book. There are no chants or mantras to perform, no affirmations to speak, or visualizations to visualize to make success materialize. Success is simply a result of hard work, treating people the right way, and keeping your eyes on the ultimate prize. Successful people from all over the world and from various cultures and ethnic groups have been practicing these attributes for centuries. In its simplest form, it boils down to faith, hard work, and doing the right thing.

I hope this book will re-invigorate your life. I sincerely hope it will touch each of you in a special way and enhance the overall quality of your life as well as mine. Hopefully it will assist you in re-evaluating your quest for success and possibly inspire and encourage you to stay the course toward success. Sometimes the journey toward success moves at a glacier's pace; sometimes things move quickly.

Sometimes we will feel so insignificant and unappreciated. However, the story of Joseph proves that there is a constant and cosmic force behind our quest for success. We may become discouraged and defeated at the course our lives take, but Joseph's story is there to remind us we are never alone or forsaken.

Lastly, this project has been an opportunity to fulfill a life-time goal of writing a book. Additionally, it has been an opportunity for me to explore my life, my goals, and what I perceive to be success and fulfillment. I am still learning every day. My journey toward true success is a continual effort. I have made my share of mistakes, committed my share of sins, and done everything wrong that could possibly be done wrong. Through it all, a faithful and gracious God has continued to pour his mercy and blessings upon me. I do not claim to be perfect, and these attributes are as much a stretch for me as they are for anyone else. If nothing else, writing this book has revealed to me my many shortcomings. I am still a work in process. However, I have come to believe that by studying, researching, and writing about these attributes, I am becoming a more complete creation. Now, let's explore the life of Joseph.

Attribute I

Spiritual Maturity

Genesis 39:2-4 *The Lord was with Joseph, and he prospered, and he lived in the house of his Egyptian master. When his master saw that the Lord was with him and that the Lord gave him success in everything he did, Joseph found favor in his eyes and became his attendant. Potiphar put him in charge of his household, and he entrusted to his care everything he owned.*

It is very apparent from Joseph's responses to challenges in his life that he had a close relationship with God. While Joseph came from a dysfunctional family by any standard, he also came from a long lineage of faithful men and women. This is not to suggest that you must be raised in a Christian or "Godly" home to experience a close relationship with God, but it is only reasonable to assume that Joseph observed and was taught the fundamentals of a close relationship with God by his parents.

A good definition of maturity is "reaching a full or developed state, generally learned, not intuitive." Yes, I believe we are born with an intuitive knowledge of God, but we must come to know him through a relationship just as we come to know and understand other human beings through relationships. Upon reflection, I am astounded at how long I have been a Christian and yet possessed such a limited understanding of God's nature. I can only blame myself for the limitations of my understanding of God because I did not commit the time to prayer, reading God's word, and coming to know him as I should have.

1

But how does one come to spiritual maturity? Does it take a lifetime to develop spiritual maturity? Obviously not, Joseph proved that spiritual maturity can be acquired at a young age, or at any age for that matter. It is never too late to make a concerted effort to come closer to God, seek a better understanding of him, and to strengthen our spiritual maturity. Developing spiritual maturity, or coming to know God and his nature better, will allow us to achieve clarity regarding God's role in our lives. We can only achieve maturity through an investment of time and a commitment to diligent prayer, bible study, and meditation. We must seek and desire God's presence in our lives.

From an early age, it is very evident Joseph trusted God and his presence in his life. Needless to say, Joseph's time was a different era. While life was surely harsh and demanding, void of the luxuries of our time, it must have been a quieter time, with fewer distractions and less white noise to steal our attention. I can only imagine that people of that era spent more time concentrating, reflecting, praying, and meditating on scripture as it existed then. These practices are imperative to achieving spiritual maturity.

I realized while writing this book and reflecting on spiritual maturity that I have spent most of my Christian walk molding God into what I wanted him to be. For many years, I viewed my relationship with God as a "quid pro quo." I would promise to be obedient if he would give me what I wanted. I would turn to him only when I was worried about something or if I wanted something to happen or not happen. I viewed God as a cosmic genie that I called upon when I wanted a promotion, a new job, or if I was concerned or stressed out about something. That view, no one's fault but my own, was indicative of my spiritual immaturity. I began to focus more on a true relationship with God, gathering a better understanding of his sovereignty in my life.

Achieving a level of spiritual maturity and understanding God's role in our lives does not happen overnight. We must make a continual, conscious, and intentional effort to learn about God's nature and his sovereignty. Quite frankly, to get to know someone, you have to spend time with them. We achieve this by prayerfully seeking his wisdom, peace, and guidance. Possessing spiritual maturity, aspiring for sanctification, and constantly striving to be better followers in all aspects of our lives will certainly make integrating the attributes of Joseph much easier. I challenge you, and I challenge myself daily, to work diligently toward a higher level of spiritual maturity. By doing so, we make life much more enjoyable, and I am confident we can achieve a higher level of success, fulfillment, and purpose.

In my opinion, achieving spiritual maturity is much like any other endeavor; we get out of it what we put into it. Just like any other relationship, our relationship with God will progress in proportion to the efforts we exert. So, there is no specific time-frame required to achieve spiritual maturity. Joseph apparently achieved a very deep level of spiritual maturity by the time he was in his teens, and his clarity regarding God, and who God is, served him well. Regardless of our age or where we are in life, it is never too late to elevate our spiritual maturity.

I believe we can experience spiritual "atrophy" just as we can experience muscular atrophy or mental atrophy. Our relation-ship with God must be exercised, massaged, and expanded to prevent a stale relationship. Working toward spiritual maturity should be a constant, life-long pursuit. Certainly, when we have a closer relationship with God, true success is experienced.

There are things that happen in life that we struggle with. If we do not possess spiritual maturity, these events, or lack of events, can undermine our existence, and in worse cases, destroy us. Let's explore how Joseph dealt with some of life's mysteries.

When Prayers Are Not Answered

I think back to 1999 when my father was diagnosed with stage four cancer. I prayed constantly for his physical healing. Day after day, week after week, month after month, I prayed for him to be delivered from this horrible disease. Yet, he continued to deteri-orate. After a lengthy battle, he succumbed to the disease, and I simply concluded that God had not answered my prayers.

For a time, I was bitter toward God. I could not understand why he did not hear my prayers. Frankly, there were some times I truly questioned whether I even believed in God anymore. How could a loving God let someone so kind and so gentle go through something so painful? How could my mother, who loved my father so dearly, be subjected to such a painful experience?

Many years later, I looked back on those difficult, dark times, and I recognized that God was involved in that situation and did answer many prayers. No, he did not physically heal my father from cancer on this earth. Dad had to face that season of life that we will all face ultimately. While God did not cure my father, he brought some dear people into our family's circle of influence for that very difficult time.

My father became re-acquainted with an old friend who was going through a similar situation. This friend turned out to be a tremendous source of encouragement to Dad during those last months. As a matter of fact, this friend had some very important discussions with Dad regarding his salvation, conversations that I had not been comfortable to have with my father. One of my uncles drove Dad to countless doctor's appointments and treatments, and he was a constant companion for him when my mother and I had to work. He spent countless hours with Dad encouraging him and talking with him. I made a new friend at work that was a tremendous source of encouragement and comfort during this difficult time. My wife and daughter gave me the love and support I needed to navigate through a painful period in my life. I cannot imagine facing that difficult chapter in my life without those people in my life. It is almost as if God set these relationships up just for that season of life. So yes, God was greatly involved in that situation. It was not the outcome I had hoped for, but now I look back and realize how blessed I was for many reasons.

I also realized as I got older how blessed I was to have my father in my life for thirty-seven years. I know a lot of people who lost their parents when they were much younger; some in the teens, some in their early twenties. I am so grateful that Dad was able to see me get married, become a father, and experience success in the workplace. I truly believe he departed this life sensing that he had fulfilled his purpose.

If I had not had my father in my life during my teens and early twenties, my life may have taken a vastly different direction. Because of the respect I had for him, and because we were very close, and because of his positive influence in my life, I was able to stay on course, despite some detours along the way. Additionally, during that last year of his life, when he was so sick, I experienced the privilege, honor, and opportunity to give back so much of what I owed to Dad. For so many years, I needed my dad. As he neared the end of his journey in life, he needed me.

Yes, God was involved in that difficult time, but I could not recognize it until much later. Now, as I am older and wiser, I realize God answered many prayers during that time. He gave my mother and I, and my brother, the grace to get through the most difficult time in our lives. He surrounded us with loving friends and family who cried and hurt right along with us.

Shortly after my father passed away, I accepted a job in Nashville, and we re-located to middle Tennessee. This change in life was at the perfect time. As a family, we were so focused on the new job, the new house, our daughter's new school, and the new city we lived in, that it took my mind off of the painful experiences from the year before. Had this opportunity arisen during my dad's illness, I possibly would have had to pass on it. In the end, God provided and led us through this difficult time. We must have spiritual maturity and perspective to recognize God's divine intervention in life, even when it appears he has abandoned us. Often, it is not until much later that we realize he was there all along.

Joseph grasped this concept at an early age. He knew and trusted that God was with him because he was spiritually mature. I did not recognize this at the time, because frankly, I was not where I needed to be spiritually. I had not spent the time getting to know the true nature of God and his involvement in my life.

Sanctification

This may sound like one of those lofty, rigid, religious words, but the basic definition of sanctification is a focused effort and intentional process to become more "Christ-like." It is a foundational Christian precept. As believers, we are instructed and encouraged throughout scripture to work at becoming more "Christ-like" or "God-like" throughout the course of our lives. If we are not changing and improving as humans and as a result of God in our lives, then we need to do some serious evaluating.

I think it is crucial to our success, fulfillment, and purpose in life for us to be constantly working toward sanctification. As Christians, we know that God will not tolerate sin. When we commit sin, he departs from us. Thus, we should be making every effort all of the time to eliminate sin in our lives. Certainly, we will never be perfect. However, if we evaluate our spiritual lives now to where we used to be, we should see quantifiable evidence that we are improving. If we want to build a meaningful, rich relationship with God, we must truly focus on eliminating behaviors in our lives that separate us from God.

Most of us can identify certain weaknesses or distractions that we have struggled with, and have bad habits that we just cannot seem to break away from. For us to experience the level of success that Joseph achieved, we need to examine our lives, determine what those dividers are, and focus on eliminating those obstacles in our lives.

Throughout this journey, I have certainly identified sin weaknesses in my life, and I am prayerfully working at eliminating them. Do I continue to fail in these areas of weaknesses? Certainly, but we must continue to work toward becoming "Christ-like" so we can experience a real and present relationship with God.

Over the years, I have observed many men and women who were strong in their faith. I always longed to be like them, but I had resigned myself to the fact that it was not possible for me to achieve that level of commitment. But as I examine what it is that separates their walk from mine, it is almost always the fact that they are truly pursuing closeness or a oneness with God.

As we whittle away at these weaknesses, God will stay close to us, and we will be able to achieve the communion and communication with God that is necessary to achieve Joseph's level of success.

God's Timing

I have always struggled with God's timing opposed to my timing. In retrospect, the reason there has been such a disconnect between what I perceived God's timing should be and what God thought it should be was simply due to my spiritual immaturity. There have been times in life when I sought an answer to a challenge and could not understand for the life of me why God took so long to answer. The story of Joseph proves that we must be patient and realize that God knows when to reveal things to us, if he chooses to reveal certain things at all. After Joseph interpreted the dreams of the baker, and specifically asked him to remember him when he reported back to the king, he languished in prison for two more years. It was not until Pharaoh was struggling with the significance of his two dreams that the baker remembered Joseph and mentioned him to Pharaoh. It is evident that God knew when to bring Joseph to Pharaoh. It is only reasonable to assume that Joseph accepted God's timing and stood ready to act when called upon. Once again, this affirms Joseph's level of spiritual maturity.

In 1993, there was a job opening in the credit card center of the bank I worked for. This was an enviable position for me. The job opening was for the "Correspondent Banking-Vice President" role. This person called on community banks in the region to do their credit card business with our bank. It involved traveling, entertaining clients and prospects, taking clients and prospects to play golf, and attending banking conventions, and included many other wonderful perks. I had worked in an operational role in the department for almost two years, and I envisioned myself being the perfect candidate for this job. I applied for the job through the internal posting process. A couple of days later, the division head called me to his office for an interview. Toward the end of the discussion, he indicated that although he thought I would be a good candidate for the role in the future, he did not think I was quite ready for the role. As a matter of fact, he already had a candidate in mind and was preparing to offer her the role.

I prayed incessantly over the next few days that this opportunity would come to pass for me, but it did not. The lady accepted the role and did a great job for a couple of years. Needless to say, I was disappointed that I did not get the job and questioned why God did not answer that prayer. However, roughly a year later in 1994, another opportunity opened up in the department that involved calling on local clients for their credit card processing business. I accepted this job and did very well at it. As fate would have it, in September of 1996, the lady who had taken the correspondent sales role accepted a role at another bank.

This time, management approached me about taking the role, which I accepted with much excitement. In looking back, I realize now that I was not really ready for that job in 1993. Had I gotten the job, I might have failed and short-circuited my career path in that arena. However, by 1996, I was prepared and ready for the role. God knew when to open that opportunity for me. He did answer my prayer, but by his timing and not mine.

Spiritual "S.W.O.T." Analysis

If you work in marketing or sales, you may be familiar with a "S.W.O.T." analysis. We should regularly conduct a "S.W.O.T." regarding our spiritual relationship with God. If you are not familiar with this acronym, it stands for strengths, weaknesses, opportunities, and threats. Businesses conduct S.W.O.T. analysis to evaluate the strength of their business or company compared to others in the marketplace. We should do the same regarding our relationship with God.

What are the strengths in my life spiritually? What can I do to enhance these strengths or to deploy my strengths? What are the weaknesses in my life? What am I doing to eradicate these weaknesses in my life? What are the opportunities in my spiritual life? What are the threats in my spiritual life? Regularly examining these facets of our spiritual walk will keep us on a path toward a more enriching and meaningful relationship with God, and will ultimately help us achieve spiritual maturity.

For the sake of transparency, some of my strengths include compassion, a spirit for serving, and good listening skills. I love to encourage others, empower others, and I love to see people smile. Some of my weaknesses include being judgmental; in other words, I often make conclusions about others based on their outward appearance before I really get to know them. Additionally, I am often opinionated and regularly make comments without thinking of the ramifications of these opinions. I can be selfish, I can be prideful, and I have a temper at times. Opportunities for me are that I come into contact with a lot of different people. I travel a lot and meet a lot of different people in various walks of life. I have a tremendous opportunity to minister to others in a one-on-one setting. Additionally, as a traveling salesman, I have somewhat of a flexible schedule. I have been blessed financially and have the opportunity to help many causes.

Threats for me include pride and the tendency to think I am responsible for the good things that have happened in my life when I know God is the source of the blessings in my life. Greed is a threat for me. I am like most other people; I like to accumulate wealth and material belongings. I must constantly remind myself that these things will rust, rot, fall away, and they have no eternal value.

When Bad Things Happen to Good People

One of the oldest mysteries of mankind is why bad things happen to good people, why good things happen to bad people, and why it seems that good people struggle to survive in a vicious world that appears to punish the righteous and reward the indignant.

Let me tell you the true story of a modern day "Job." Robert was born into a large family in southern Florida in 1937. He discovered a passion for the vocation that would forever change his life at a young age and moved to Alabama in the early 1960s. He married a young lady he fell in love with and started a family. From these humble beginnings, Robert and Judy began chasing their dreams. As fate would have it, he was very successful in his particular field. Robert and his wife, Judy, had three children; two sons and one daughter. Through the 1960s, 1970s, and most of the 1980s Robert and Judy's life was one blessed with success, happiness, and abundance. By the late 1980s, they had reached the pinnacle of life and success. A stellar career had materialized for Robert, and the couple's three children were experiencing success in their own right. It seemed a secure, happy, and successful future lie ahead of them.

However, in the late 1980s, Robert and Judy's life would begin to take some crazy and tragic turns. First, Robert was involved in a serious automobile accident in Pennsylvania in June of 1988. He suffered both debilitating physical injuries and serious brain injuries that would require months of intense rehabilitation. Nonetheless, Robert committed to the strenuous requirements of the rehabilitation and vowed to return to his previous strength. Unfortunately, he would soon find that precious lifelong memories had been erased from his mind and are still absent to this day. Additionally, Robert's successful career came to an end due to that accident.

Unbelievably, just four years later, in 1992, his youngest son, Clifford, twenty-seven years old at the time, was also injured in a tragic automobile accident in Michigan. Sadly, Cliff's injuries would prove to be fatal. Robert and Judy struggled to cope with the tragic turn their lives had taken. Surely, life could not deal a more dreadful blow.

Shockingly, on July 13, 1993, their oldest son, David, was involved in a freak helicopter crash near Birmingham, Alabama. The crash would take the life of their oldest and only remaining son and critically injure a life-long friend. Needless to say, Robert and Judy were crushed by this final and cruel tragedy in their lives. Then, incredibly, on February 11 of 1994, a longtime friend, business associate, and protégé of Robert's was also killed in a car wreck in Florida.

Sadly, in 1996, Robert and his wife Judy had to auction off much of their private property, including priceless and personal belongings, in an effort to satisfy a stack of debts incurred from his accident and the treatments and rehabilitation that followed. Eventually, Robert and Judy had to file bankruptcy. Later in 1996, after thirty-six years of marriage, Robert and Judy filed for divorce. The crushing burdens of their losses proved too much to bear for the couple. After all of the success, and then all of the tragedy, they decided to go their separate ways. This story may sound unbelievable, but it is absolutely true.

Robert, to those of us who keep up with the sport of NASCAR racing, is "Bobby" Allison. "Bobby" Allison, a key member of the "Alabama Gang" of stock car drivers, is one of the most successful drivers in the history of the sport. He won eighty-four races during his career, and he won the coveted Daytona 500 three times. Additionally, Bobby won the 1983 "Winston Cup," the most envious award in all of stock car racing. Bobby Allison experienced tremendous success throughout his career, and his two sons were following in their father's footsteps.

Robert, or "Bobby" as race fans know him, was critically injured at the Pocono Pennsylvania race track in June of 1988. In 1992, his son, Clifford, wrecked and died while qualifying for a race at the Michigan International raceway. Just a year later, his oldest son, "Davey," an up-and-coming driver in the Winston Cup series who had won numerous races in his short career, crashed a helicopter at the Talladega speedway near Birmingham, Alabama while attempting to land with lifelong family friend "Red" Farmer on board. "Red" was critically injured, but would eventually recover, but "Davey" died from his injuries a short time later. The family friend, who died in the car wreck in Florida, was Neal Bonnett, another member of the "Alabama Gang." He wrecked and died during a practice session at Daytona in February of 1994.

Judy and Bobby divorced in 1996, but in an amazing display of renewal and recommitment, the couple re-married in 2000. After everything they had been through, despite the heartbreak and adversity, they decided they needed to finish the most important race of their lives together. Both acknowledged that the death of their two sons had taken a significant toll on their marriage. On May 17, 2011, after being inducted to the NASCAR Hall of Fame, Robert "Bobby" Allison stated the following:

"I feel life is tough. Everybody has had good times and bad times. Some people have had really bad times, and some have had more bad times than others. I feel like we put our effort in. We had some success that we're really proud of, so anytime the deal comes up, I'd rather think about the successful part. You don't have to like what happens, but you have to accept it. I accept it and go on to whatever the next deal is. I know people that have lost children to disease and highway crashes, those kinds of things. Same thing. It's something you really, really wish didn't happen, but you have to accept it."

The really tragic part of Bobby's story is that he cannot remember his 1988 Daytona 500 win, perhaps his most memorable. In this race, he finished first, and his son, Davey, finished second, and they cried and hugged at victory lane.

Considering everything this family went through, I look at this summary as a fair assessment of life and what can happen. We do not know what waits around the corner for us. We are not guaranteed anything. This is the story of an ordinary family who had everything and then lost it all; not because of anything they did or did not do, but simply because of this world we live in.

Joseph was dealt some poor circumstances when he really did not deserve them. We have all been dealt some poor circumstances when we did not deserve them. However, Joseph chose to plow on and honor God despite the tragic turn of events in his life. We will never know this side of heaven why things happen the way they do. We will never understand how the dictators of nations can execute millions of people with no hint of remorse or regret. We will never understand how mankind can stand by while thousands of people starve to death everyday in rotting third-world countries. We cannot comprehend the meaning of life when we see a story on the local news about children who have been left in a hot car in the middle of the summer, only to suffocate to death. We can only trust that God is in control and in charge. One day, we will understand it all, but until then, we can only do as Joseph did and plow on.

Seasons of Waiting

Joseph surely experienced frustration, anxiety, and discouragement during those dark times of waiting in his life. We have all experienced periods in our lives where we seem to be stuck in a rut. Nothing appears to be happening as we envisioned it would. Genesis hints at Joseph's anguish while in prison when he asks the baker to remember him when he is sent back to Pharaoh. It is only natural for us to want things to happen quickly. How we utilize these times of waiting can be crucial in our quest for success.

Joseph referred to the prison he was in as a dungeon. One commentary I read suggests that Joseph was likely being held in a minimum security prison where the prisoners "of the Pharaoh" were held. Regardless of whether it was a country club prison or Alcatraz, it was still confinement. Joseph was discouraged, frustrated, and depressed during this time of waiting.

I have certainly experienced these seasons of waiting many times in my life: Waiting for the right person to come along that I wanted to spend my life with, waiting for that promotion that seemed to go to everyone else, waiting for a health condition of a loved one to improve. The lists can go on and on. Those who have a higher level of spiritual maturity stand a better chance of waiting through these periods with grace and peace. They tend to utilize this time of waiting in a much more positive way. If we possess a better understanding of God and his character, we will understand that we view things through a temporal lens while God views events through an eternal lens.

Admittedly, this aspect of my faith walk has been one of my biggest struggles. I, by nature, am a very impatient person. I like to see things happen quickly. I lose interest in things if they move too slowly. However, God has taught me that my timeline is not his timeline. I cannot even begin to comprehend his design, intelligence, and divine order in all things. Thus, I am learning to let go and let him reveal when he is ready.

A few months ago, our pastor gave a very timely message regarding seasons of waiting. He pointed out that seasons of waiting are normal in our lives, just as they were in Joseph's life. He also pointed out that we should:

- pray while waiting
- obey while waiting
- fellowship with others while waiting
- prepare while waiting

We should always remember that times of waiting are times to prepare for what lies ahead. These periods of time should not be viewed as a time of inactivity. Joseph certainly used these "down" times between significant events and success in his life to prepare for the next opportunity or challenge. While we are waiting for great things to happen, we should be preparing ourselves for that greater responsibility as I believe Joseph did.

As I mentioned earlier, by nature, I am a very impatient person. I like to see things happen quickly. However, over the last several years, God has taught me much regarding waiting. The economic collapse in 2008 has taught me patience through times of uncertainty. As I write this book, my seventy-year-old mother has been working through some health issues and has been seeking an answer for over a year. She has seen doctor after doctor with little success in identifying the cause of the issues and how to resolve it.

I do not believe God causes these events to teach me patience, but rather I believe he uses these events to teach me patience. Understanding and accepting seasons of waiting has been a lifelong quest for me. I certainly feel that I deal with these periods much better than I used to, although I will admit I still struggle with times of waiting. We should pray for discernment, courage, and clarity from God while working through these times of our lives, and understand that everyone faces seasons of waiting.

Quiet Times

I am an absolute believer in the positive effects that spending quiet time alone can,have on an individual. I began doing this back in the mid 1990s. It is absolutely crucial that we carve out fifteen to thirty minutes a day, morning or night, to spend some time alone, concentrating on our goals, past successes, our purpose, and fulfillment. You can spend this time praying, meditating, visualizing successes and goals, reading scripture, or simply spending some time in the quietness. Our world is inundated with constant distractions. It may take some time to train your brain to slow down and focus on something for extended periods of time. However, the benefits are immeasurable. Whether you call it meditating, praying, or whatever, spending a few minutes alone and focusing on your goals, tasks, God, whatever, helps reset and re-focus your mind. There are countless apps for smart phones that are designed to help you relax, focus, and visualize. Try doing this for a month and see how it can enrich your life.

I began meditating, visualizing, and using affirmations in 1996. Honestly, I was skeptical about the supposed benefits of these practices. However, after a short period of time, I recognized an increase in my confidence, clarity, focus, and self-esteem. I began affirming and visualizing certain goals and desires, and amazingly they seemed to come to fruition, not because these practices are magical or mystical, but because thinking of and visualizing these goals, actions and results keep us focused on what needs to be done to achieve them.

Ask anyone who knows me, and they will tell you I am a huge Florida Gators fan. In 1996, Danny Wuerffel led the Gators to their first football national championship, and he also won the Heisman trophy that same season. I read in a magazine article that Wuerffel, in addition to working out, practicing, and throwing routes with his receivers, also practiced visualizations as part of his preparation regimen. He said in this article that he would visualize in his mind his receivers running their routes, he would visualize himself dropping back in the pocket, and he would visualize the pass being thrown in perfect timing to the receiver. He was a firm believer that visualizations were an important part of his preparation and that it contributed to his success. I agree. There is nothing mystical or magical about visualizing. It is a process of previewing a success before it happens, and it prepares us for that success.

In the end, developing spiritual maturity equips and enables us to thrust through those challenging times in our lives. It is not so much about understanding God's sovereignty in our lives, but rather accepting his sovereignty in our lives. I have come to realize that there are many things that happen in the world that I do not understand and never will in this temporal world. Perhaps on the other side we will understand why things happen the way they do.

Equally, developing spiritual maturity equips and enables us to thrust through those times of great success in our lives when we are equally vulnerable. Experiencing great success can be dangerous. We tend to think we are responsible for our success rather than God. We sometimes become complacent after great success and develop a sense of invincibility. We may become careless regarding moral trip wires in our lives. Continually developing and possessing spiritual maturity keeps us on an even keel. Likewise, increasing our spiritual maturity makes the other attributes easier to obtain because they work together. Spend some time evaluating your life and where you are spiritually, fill in the gaps of weakness, and prepare for what God has in store for you. Joseph could not have weathered the peaks and valleys in his life, and achieved what he achieved, without a true understanding and acceptance of God's sovereignty in his life.

Attribute II

Integrity/Character/Ethics

Genesis 39:6-10 *So he left in Joseph's care everything he had; with Joseph in charge, he did not concern himself with anything except the food he ate. Now Joseph was well-built and handsome, and after a while his master's wife took notice of Joseph and said "Come to bed with me!" But he refused. "With me in charge, my master does not concern himself with anything in the house; everything he owns he has entrusted to my care. No one is greater in this house than I am. My master has withheld nothing from me except you, because you are his wife. How then could I do such a wicked thing and sin against God?"*

A consistent theme throughout the story of Joseph is this. Joseph always "obtained favor" with those he knew. What does it mean to obtain favor? Not only did Potiphar, the prison captain, and Pharaoh like Joseph, which they obviously did, but they trusted him immensely. Through his actions, thoughts, and behaviors, he convinced those he came into contact with to hand responsibility over to him. While I think possessing all of the attributes played a role in Joseph gaining favor, I think he consistently gained favor because he unfailingly always did what was right. When you always do what is right, people notice, and responsibility and "favor" ensue.

Certainly Joseph sinned and battled his own weaknesses like anyone else. Nowhere in scripture is it implied that Joseph was supernatural or that he possessed any powers above that of a

16

regular human. However, in evaluating Joseph's life, it is obvious that Joseph was committed to doing what was right. By doing what was right, Joseph inevitably earned the trust of those around him.

When his father wanted to know what his brothers were up to, he asked Joseph to check on them because he knew Joseph would do what was right and report back to him. After acquiring Joseph from the slave traders, Potiphar put Joseph in charge of his household because he trusted him. When Joseph was thrown into prison, the prison master put him in charge of all the duties in the prison because he trusted Joseph.

After Joseph interpreted the dreams of Pharaoh, the king put him in charge of all of Egypt, second in authority only to Pharaoh, because he trusted him. Genesis points out that Pharaoh gave Joseph his signet ring and robe. This was a symbol of validation, authority, and confidence. Throughout his life, Joseph earned responsibility, authority, and success by being trustworthy.

Integrity

One only needs to read the recent newspapers to see what happens when those in authority usurp or abuse their power and abandon integrity, ethics, and morals. Volumes could be written about the CEOs, CFOs, and other executives who have went to prison for fraud or who drove their businesses into bankruptcy by being dishonest, unethical, and greedy. Ken Lay of Enron, Dennis Kozlowski of Tyco, Bernard Ebbers of Worldcom, and Bernie Madoff are just a few recent examples of powerful men who fell from grace and destroyed great companies by compromising character and integrity.

We can read almost daily about politicians, athletes, and others in power who have committed adultery, accepted bribes, committed crimes, or compromised ethics. In many cases, it is likely that these people started out on the right path to success. They may have possessed all of the attributes needed for true success in the beginning. But somewhere along the way, they began to drift away from the attributes. A subtle compromise here and there, a slight deviation from the path along the way, then, as we begin to skirt the lines of right and wrong, our conscience begins to dull, and we build up a tolerance for wrong, or we begin to rationalize our actions, right or wrong.

Likewise, we should always remember, just because something may be legal, we cannot always assume it is right or ethical. There have been numerous examples of people choosing an action or inaction and getting away with it legally, even though they knew, or at least suspected, it was unethical or immoral. What may begin as a slight, benign flirtation with unethical behavior will eventually lead to all out adultery against morals, ethics, and character. Never compromise what is right. We usually possess an intuitive receiver that picks up a signal when we are wondering if an action or inaction is right or wrong. Trust that signal and do not be tempted to take the wrong path.

I heard a pastor make a comment a few months ago that I thought was very compelling. He said, and I am paraphrasing, that a nation's number of laws will generally mirror the moral code of that society or nation. In other words, if there has to be thousands of laws to spell out everything that is wrong and right to the people, then that society struggles with recognizing wrong from right. While much is spoken regarding morals, ethics, and integrity in our society, our behavior is often the opposite. This is not a platform to harp on our national morals, ethics, and character, or lack of them. We can only control our own lives and influence those we come into contact with by being an example. Then, hopefully, we will inspire others to follow our example.

Despite the many pitfalls thrown in Joseph's path, there is no indication that he ever considered compromising his integrity. As a matter of fact, every verse seems to emphasize Joseph's unshakable commitment to doing what was right. This must have been difficult. There must have been times when Joseph felt that "no good deed goes unpunished." However, Joseph was unyielding in his commitment to integrity, character, and his code of ethics.

While the author of Genesis does not indicate this, I have wondered if Potiphar really even believed the allegations against Joseph regarding the attempted attack on his wife. I think if Potiphar had believed Joseph attacked his wife, he would have had Joseph executed. However, I think Potiphar had to have

Joseph incarcerated in an effort to maintain his dignity and to appease his wife.

Whether it was Potiphar, the head of the prison guard, or the King of Egypt, all of these men recognized Joseph's commitment to integrity, and they gave him authority and responsibility over much. If people trust you, they will ask you to take responsibility for tasks and projects. Thus, it is crucial to build integrity into your life. Genesis chapter 39:6 also states that Potiphar "Left all that he had in Joseph's charge, and because of him (Joseph), he had no concern about anything but the food he ate." Not only did Potiphar put Joseph in charge of everything, he did not even feel the need to check up on him. That's how much Potiphar trusted him.

Later, when Pharaoh put Joseph second in command, he adorned him with a "signet" ring. While this was likely a ceremonial procedure, I suspect Pharaoh had another motive in mind. I believe he gave the ring to Joseph to illustrate to the rest of Egypt that he trusted Joseph and trusted in his wisdom. Pharaoh wanted no one to question or second guess his trust and confidence in Joseph. I am sure there were some well-deserving, loyal Egyptians who may have been insulted that a young Hebrew foreigner was put in charge before them. I am sure that many had served Pharaoh faithfully through the years. However, Pharaoh put the issue to rest by giving the signet ring to Joseph. This particular Pharaoh was obviously a good judge of character and good at spotting potential. Additionally, even though Egyptians had their own forms of religion, it is obvious that Pharaoh recognized Joseph's divine intuitiveness. His ability to translate Pharaoh's dreams with such clarity and confidence moved Pharaoh.

Another important aspect to Joseph's success is this. He never undermined others or used "cutthroat" tactics to advance his position of authority or responsibility. From every indication, Joseph achieved his success through sincere and honest efforts. Genesis never hints that Joseph attempted to usurp authority or undermine those he served or reported to. He gained success the old fashioned way, he earned it. Over the years, I have seen numerous careers derailed because these people tried to circumvent the normal chain of command, or tried to undermine those ahead of them in an effort to ascend more rapidly. We should always respect authority and trust that God will put the rungs of the ladder before us in his due time.

Joseph fully understood the chain of authority and how the law of authority applied in the family, the workplace, and the government. Joseph recognized the need for managerial hierarchy, and although he knew he would one day serve in a leader's role, he never approached his responsibilities with a sense of arrogance or superiority. He simply accepted delegation and responsibility from those he reported to and respected their position.

The successes that Joseph experienced were a result of hard work, pure and honest motivations, and a sincere eagerness to accomplish what was laid before him. For us to experience true success and fulfillment, I firmly believe we must humbly respect the authority that has been placed ahead of us. Like Joseph, we need to recognize that our leaders and superiors are there to mentor, teach, and guide us on our path to success. Observing wise and more experienced superiors gives us insight and wisdom we will need when we are presented with opportunities in their given time.

Character

Jim Rohn, a well known motivational speaker, states that, "Character is not something you are born with, and it is not something that cannot be changed." In other words, it is not like our fingerprints or the color of our eyes. While our environment, society, and culture may play a significant role in the development of our character, ultimately, we chisel and craft our character through our actions and reactions to life events. As Mr. Rohn also added, "You build character by how you respond to what happens in your life, whether it's winning every game, losing every game, getting rich, or dealing with hard times."

Through pure dependence on and trust in God, Joseph was able to develop positive, exemplary character through the adversities he faced. We should always be evaluating our character and making sure our actions, thoughts, and behavior are indicative of "God-like" character.

In banking, lenders look at what is referred to as the four "C's" of a borrower when evaluating or making a potential loan. These four "C's" are:

- **Credit** – the actual credit history or borrowing history of the borrower.
- **Cash flow** – does the borrower's revenues cover the anticipated debt load?
- **Collateral** – would the value of the collateral cover the loan balance if needed?
- **Character** – how will the borrower react if everything else goes wrong?

I have had bankers tell me that they have looked at loans where the borrower's credit, cash flow, and collateral position all fit the parameters of their lending matrix, but they passed on the loan because of suspect or questionable character of the borrower. I have had bankers tell me that they have made loans to folks whose credit, cash flow, and collateral were marginal, but because their character was impeccable, they still made the loan. Character is crucial to our success.

Allowing God to develop and hone our character throughout our lives will prepare us to meet our challenges and opportunities in a positive and constructive way. It is evident that Joseph recognized this principle at a very young age. Had Joseph's character not been square with God's, his life could have easily taken a downhill spiral, and he would not have had the impact that God intended for him. We will all face obstacles in our lives. While they may not be identical to the obstacles Joseph faced, they will be just as defining. We can only hope to face these hurdles with grace and wisdom if we allow God to chisel our character.

Trustworthiness

Certainly possessing integrity and character is crucial for us to achieve success. Equally as important is being trustworthy. Being trustworthy means you can be counted on to be there, to carry your load. It is being dependable and reliable. It also means giving your best effort in every task presented. Integrity, character, and trustworthiness complement each other, but possessing all three traits is critical to success in our professional pursuits, spiritual pursuits, and in our relationships, both professionally and personally. Joseph reflected each of these important traits in his life, and everyone noticed that he was special.

Sadly, a few years ago, I was reminded of the fragility of trustworthiness and credibility. I had spent several years calling on clients in a new territory and had worked hard to build a good reputation in that market based on my integrity and trustworthiness. Sadly, when the recession hit in 2008, the bank I worked for failed and was taken over by the FDIC. Because of the failure, the stock in the bank was rendered worthless. The stockholders of the bank, many of them good customers and good friends, took a significant financial loss.

While I was not personally responsible for the failure of the bank, and even though I had no idea the bank would ultimately be closed, these trusting friends and clients looked to me for guidance and advice on investing in this company. Because I did not see the trouble coming, I felt my credibility was tainted. Sadly, the experience strained some relationships, and quite frankly, ended some relationships that I viewed as very valuable. This experience was one of the darkest times of my career, and I struggled with guilt and discouragement for a couple of years. Trustworthiness takes time and hard work to build. It only takes one slip up to destroy it, and it is extremely hard, if not impossible sometimes, to gain it back. Fortunately, I have been able to put those mistakes behind me and move on.

Look at the company you work for and the people you surround yourself with. Would the company you work for ever ask you to do anything unethical or something you do not feel comfortable or right doing? Every action, no matter how large or how small, has an impact. That impact will either be a positive reflection on your character, integrity, and trustworthiness, or a negative reflection on your reputation. Never discount the value of a decision. Every one, no matter how large or small, produces ramifications.

Let me speak in banker's terms. In all of our relationships, both professionally and personally, we build a certain amount of "trust equity." It can take years to build "trust equity," but it can be destroyed quickly with one bad decision, choice, action, or inaction. Once that "trust equity" is destroyed, it is very difficult to restore. Sadly, even if it is restored, it is often very difficult to restore it to its original value.

In my twenty plus years of sales, I have known many salespeople who have had the reputation of saying or doing anything to get the sale. Sometimes, their actions bordered on unethical or skirted the boundaries of business ethics. Generally speaking, these salespeople may experience some level of success for a short time, but ultimately they will usually fail at sales. People will eventually figure them out. For this reason, sales-people do not always have the best reputation in the business place in regards to morals, character, and ethics. Sometimes when the pressure is on, it is tempting to say what you think the potential client wants to hear to get the deal done. However, no one will be happy if down the road things are not as they were presented. I have learned through the years that you are much better off being honest and up front with prospects, and to keep expectations real.

Trust is crucial for any relationship. Whether it is in the workplace, at home with a spouse or a partner, or a casual friend-ship, we must be honest with others. I have often had people ask me about the great relationship I have with my wife. I always point out that one of the best aspects of our relationship is our trust in, and for, each other. Neither one of us has ever done anything that would warrant distrust or suspicion. Therefore, we have a wonderful marriage. I never discount the value of trust. When we first got married, I kept a separate checking account. However, I discovered after a while that this was not healthy because I did not really have to be accountable to her for where I spent my money. So we decided to combine our checking accounts into one. Not that I was doing anything shady or wrong, but we needed that transparency. Now, I have to turn over every receipt to her, and it works best that way. Likewise, she will always call me before she spends a large sum of money and make sure I am okay with it. It is the same with me. If I want a golf club, or a new musical instrument, I always discuss with her first. Our relationship is better that way.

Work Ethic

A job poorly done, no matter how mundane or insignificant, is a contradiction to what scripture teaches us about our work efforts. Joseph obviously understood that his job, regardless of what it was, was to be done well. I am amazed, and quite frankly perplexed, when I see Christians, who otherwise seem to live out their faith in other aspects, perform a job or a task poorly.

We all have those days when we are just not really into our work. We all have days when we just do not feel like putting forth our best effort. But we must always be mindful that our work, whatever it is, is a reflection of our character. Concentrating on our work with a laser-like focus will help us achieve more, accomplish much, and bring value to those for which we work. When our work, whatever it is, creates value, we will be rewarded. More importantly, our work is a testament to our faith and to our commitment to do what is right.

I believe Joseph undertook every task, whether it was watching over his father's flocks, overseeing Potiphar's household, or preparing for the catastrophic drought with intense focus and commitment. I am convinced he worked hard, expected others to work hard, and served as an example to those within his circle of influence.

We must be conscientious about our work. Once again, everything we do is a testament to our faith, either good or bad. Regardless of how mundane the task may seem, or how insignificant our work may appear, it is ultimately on display for everyone to see our efforts and results. I sense that Joseph perceived his work as an opportunity to shine and a chance to represent the God he loved, served, and trusted. Never think that a below average or below par performance will suffice. Never think that no one is watching your efforts. Someone is always watching and observing what we do, and they will either applaud or criticize our efforts. If we want to be like Joseph, we must put our best effort into every task to insure no one can question our commitment to excellence.

Being conscientious about our work is very different from developing an arrogant pride about our work or our accomplishments. Being conscientious means we are grateful to have responsibility, and we recognize that God will be glorified through this task, or that someone's life may be made better by what we do. Being prideful and arrogant about our jobs or accomplishments indicates that we think we earned the responsibility and the rewards based on our own merits or capability. We should always possess a genuine gratefulness to God for entrusting us with opportunities and challenges. Keeping this type of attitude will please God and impact those you come into contact with.

Perfectionism

Being a perfectionist about everything can slow or impede our progress. I appreciate anyone who takes pride in the work, and does it right. However, perfectionism can distract us from accomplishing greater things. There have been many times where I have been obsessed with a task and finally realized that the task was really not that important in the grand scheme of things. Devote the proper time to a task to complete it correctly and then move on to the next task. There is no need for "paralysis by analysis" in everything we do.

I have observed many people over the years that possessed tremendous talent, but they could never be satisfied with their efforts, and they continued to delay their contributions to the organization because they were paralyzed by the dreaded curse of perfectionism. We need to give our best to any effort, but there comes a time when we need to give our best and move on to the next challenge. Constantly re-hashing every decision will only paralyze our efforts and impede progress.

I sense that Joseph evaluated his situation, considered the facts of the situation, made a rational decision regarding the situation, acted, and then moved on to the next challenge. We must not be afraid to act. We must trust that if we are prepared and properly informed, we will react properly to the situation at hand.

Failures

In this context, failures are very different from mistakes. The failures we discuss here are those crucial moments in our lives where we use bad judgment or commit a moral failure. Failures can range in severity and consequences. Moral failures can result in the absolute destruction of our careers, families, and sometimes even our lives. We will all experience failure in our lives. Certain failures can actually be constructive and an opportunity to improve shortcomings and weaknesses. When we fail, regardless of the significance of the failure, we should evaluate what triggered the failure and identify what we can do to eliminate and prevent that failure from occurring again. We must accept the responsibility that comes from a failure and attempt to repair the damage that results.

However, we must also understand the consequences that result from certain "moral" failures. While some failures can be overcome, and we may possibly experience restoration, it is much easier to avoid the failure altogether. For the most part, moral failures leave irreversible scars on our families, careers, relationships, and lives.

We should understand that nothing positive can be gained from constantly rehashing or re-living the failures we have experienced in life. This is different from evaluating a failure, at the time it occurred, and concentrating on what we can do different to prevent the failure from occurring again. We will discuss forgiving ourselves later in the book.

We all have areas of weaknesses in our lives. It is crucial, if we want to achieve optimum success, that we evaluate the spiritual weaknesses in our lives and put forth a concerted effort to eliminate these weaknesses. This ties back in to the spiritual maturity attribute. Once again, if we understand God, we know that he despises sin and will flee from it. When we sin, we lose the presence of God. To fully know him and understand him, we need to have him with us. As humans, we will always sin. But we should be careful and not dismiss or downplay failure just because we are human. There are ways to overcome sin if we work at it.

In this modern era we live in, moral failures can absolutely destroy our careers, marriages, friendships, and our witness for God. We must realize that all of our actions leave a digital footprint and a toxic trail. Like it or loath it, our past actions are only a "Google" search away. If you do not believe me, just search your name on the internet. You may be amazed what you can find out about yourself. Long gone are the days when you could experience a failure, move to another company, or move to another state, and no one find out about your past. You cannot outrun your past today. Modern technology has made it difficult to erase the mistakes of our past. Due to thorough background checks and pre-employment vetting, companies can now drill down into our pasts. Our track record in life, for better or for worse, is more transparent and less erasable. Moral failures can, and will, follow and haunt us for many years. The risk is just not worth taking.

Additionally, the fallout from a moral failure can wreck your marriage, your witness as a believer, and destroy the respect and credibility that you spend years building. People are willing to forgive you for innocent mistakes; everyone makes mistakes. But the fallout from a moral failure will derail your path to success and may destroy everything that is important to you.

I will never forget the sad situation where a high ranking executive of a company I worked for became involved in an inappropriate relationship with a co-worker. Ultimately, they both lost their jobs, their marriages, and their families. And he eventually committed suicide. This man and his family had sacrificed and worked hard their entire lives to achieve success, and it was all destroyed due to poor choices. The impact of these decisions will affect his family for the remainder of their lives.

I am sure he never intended for this to happen. We should never become complacent regarding potential traps in our lives. Traps and lures lurk on every corner, and they can be subtle. What may seem like an innocent, benign relationship with a co-worker can eventually turn into a failure with heart-breaking consequences. Be diligent regarding vulnerable situations and never presume you are strong enough to walk away. I believe this is why Joseph ran from Potiphar's wife when she propositioned him. He did not even want to give himself time to think about her offer.

I have seen countless marriages destroyed, careers cut short, and children impacted for life by the aftershocks of a serious moral failure. During a men's conference at our church a few months ago, our pastor held up a picture of him, his wife, and children. He said that every day he looks at that picture and thinks of the sacrifice and the hard work he and his wife has put into their marriage. He said he only has to think of the pain, disappointment, and heartbreak it would bring if he had to tell them that he had committed a moral failure. Just the thought of the potential pain reminds him to always be diligent regarding the sanctity of his family.

Oddly enough, it often seems that these catastrophic moral failures occur when a person has achieved success, and more times than not, it is a man who fails. I do not think this is coincidence. When a person is working on succeeding and achieving objectives, they tend to possess an unshakable focus. Unfortunately, once they reach the summit, it is easier to become complacent. They tend to develop an ego, and they convince themselves that they are invincible.

Additionally, successful people can become prey. There is no shortage of people looking to take advantage of successful people. Super athletes, politicians, corporate executives, and business owners can attract vultures. In some sense, the more successful we are, the larger the "bulls-eye" is on our backs.

This was true in Biblical times as well. King David, Samson, Solomon, and many others experienced their biggest failures after they had achieved tremendous success. It is easy to become complacent once we reach the top of the mountain. We tend to develop an aura of invincibility. Never fool yourself into thinking that we cannot fall from grace. It happens to people every day in every walk of life.

My wife and I have years of hard work and sacrifice into our marriage. We have that wonderful relationship because of the efforts we have put into this marriage. I could never experience these memories with anyone else. My marriage is the most important relationship I have on this earth, and I will never put myself in a position that would compromise that trust. My family is my greatest asset on this earth. I vow to protect it, defend it, and enrich it through the remainder of my days.

Failures, mistakes, and errors are unavoidable in life. If handled correctly, they can serve as valuable building blocks in our ultimate quest for success. But remember, if you do anything worth doing, you will experience failure. If you do nothing, you have already failed. Do not avoid situations out of fear of failure. Dive in, take chances, take them wisely, and chalk a mistake up for experience. Dissect a failure and determine what you can do to prevent that failure from occurring again.

Attribute III

Contentment

Genesis 39:20-21 *But while Joseph was there in the prison the Lord was with him.*

Because of Joseph's understanding of God and his unshakable trust in God, he was content. Because Joseph accepted God's sovereignty in his life, he was content. Because Joseph was confident of God's governance in his life, Joseph chose to be content. By being content no matter his circumstances, Joseph was able to excel at everything he did. Joseph comprehended that God was a protecting presence in his life. Joseph trusted God and believed with unshakable conviction that God was steering and leading his path. Because of these things, Joseph was content.

There have been times when we all have ended up in a place we hate. We may have a job that seems to be going nowhere. We may be working for a boss who is difficult. We may be enduring a financial crisis we cannot seem to overcome. Whatever the trial may be, we all have those moments when we want to be somewhere else. We may even begin to question why God would put us in that place. Joseph believed and trusted that he was where he was because God placed him there. When we are content in our surroundings, it is evident. When are not content in our surroundings, it is evident. People do, and will, notice our mood and disposition. Contentment is about being happy where you are while you are trying to get to where you want to go.

My wife and I got married a little later in life than a lot of couples I knew. Prior to our marriage, I had made some poor financial decisions and was recovering from those decisions. So when we started our life together, I compared where we were financially to where a lot of other couples our age were financially. I always felt as if I was trying to catch up with others. I was happy and somewhat content, but I always felt that if we could just hit that next level of financial security, I would be so much more content. If I could make a little more money, if we could live in a nicer neighborhood, if I already had our daughter's college paid for, I felt I could be at peace. This behavior is known as the dreaded comparison syndrome. Comparing yourself to others can, and will, lead to frustration, anxiety, and discontentment.

Finally, I had an epiphany, or perhaps God just revealed it to me (thanks to some spiritual maturity) that I better enjoy and cherish every moment I have. I finally realized that each day is precious, so why waste today wishing I had more stuff or wishing I was in a different position? Finally, I also realized that I will never have the most and I will never have the least. I realized that I was blessed and fortunate to be somewhere in between everyone else. I can truthfully say, and this is probably because of where I am in my walk with God, that I am very content right now. I have a wonderful marriage, a wonderful daughter, and a loving support group of friends, family, customers, and acquaintances.

My mother has a dear friend that she has known since they were teenagers. This friend and her husband have been very successful financially by anyone's standards. However, this lady is never content with what she has. Life is passing her by, and she is still trying to amass more in material wealth. She has wasted so many wonderful events in life because she was fixated on having more than everyone else. It is sad to think that one day she will look back on her life and wish she could relive the time she wasted on coveting more.

What is it about Americans? Despite being the most blessed nation in the history of mankind, we seem to be the most unhappy, discontented people in the world. I truly think we have lost our ability to be content in our current circumstances. Our drives, ambitions, and our impression of contentment have been so distorted. Joseph proved time and time again that you obtain contentment through proper aspirations, goals, and desires.

We are constantly inundated with advertisements for cars, boats, and other stuff that will supposedly bring us contentment. Americans have developed an insatiable appetite for stuff. One of the most successful industries in this country over the last twenty years has been the storage sector. We now have so much stuff that we have to rent storage units to keep it all. Yet, we are still not content. We fool ourselves into thinking that once we buy the bigger house, the latest gadget, a bigger car, a beach house, a mountain cabin, then surely we will be content. Yet the quest for satisfaction and fulfillment never ends.

Joseph's life was constant reminder to be content in our circumstances and trust that God is guiding our way. Joseph's story also proves that there will be unexpected setbacks in life. We have all experienced those times when it seems like everything is turned against us. We must make a conscious effort to remain content throughout these valleys of life. Some setbacks are minor in nature, and we brush them off fairly easily. Other events happen in our lives that crush our very spirit. Joseph experienced many of these setbacks, but remained resilient and, from all accounts, content.

It is only reasonable to assume that Joseph experienced sadness, frustration, and the normal emotions we all do when things do not go as we had hoped. I am sure Joseph wept when weeping was appropriate. As the Bible mentions in Proverbs, there is a time for laughing and a time for crying; happy seasons and sad seasons. God understands that we will be sad at times, especially during times of loss.

The good news is that contentment can be obtained where you are now and is just an attitude change away. Relish and savor these very moments because they are flashing by at warp speed. Each day that passes is one less day we have left. There will come a time when we wish we had them again. By not being content in the present, we are robbing ourselves of the joy God intended for us.

Contentment is an overall and overriding sense of happiness. However, once again, being content does not mean we will never be sad, heart-broken, depressed, or distraught. Tragedy and loss is a part of living in this world. Every human being who has ever lived or who will ever live will be exposed to loss and pain. If nothing else, we can take solace in the fact that tragedy does not discriminate, and does not know ethnic, race, or social boundaries.

To be content, we need to change our perspective. Instead of being bitter because of what we do not have, we should take an inventory of the abundant blessings in our lives and thank God for where we are and what we have. I look around and see so many unhappy people who really have reason to be unhappy.

Positive Attitude

Perhaps no one flaw can derail your path to success as much as a poor attitude. I have seen so many people undermine their potential and opportunities because they were adversarial or confrontational with other employees, or they're always questioning why or how things have to be done. Be cheerful, willing, and happy to do the tasks as long as they do not compromise your integrity or character. Team players always stand out to leaders and will always be called upon when opportunities arise. I sense that Joseph maintained a positive attitude in all things. I envision him willingly and gladly accepting responsibilities when given the opportunity.

When I think of my dad, I always remember that he was very content. Things did not always go the way he planned. He had some great success financially at times, and went through times when things did not work out so well. However, I never remember him complaining about anything. He was always just happy to get up and go work hard for the day, come home, eat supper with us, and do it all over again the next day.

I have not always possessed that attitude of contentment, not because I was unhappy with my relationships, but because I was always hoping to have just a little more. I have learned to be grateful for today, wherever I am, because there will come a time when I will wish I was where I am now.

Proper Perspective

Additionally, we must maintain the proper perspective on life. I truly believe Joseph possessed a "kingdom" perspective. I think he realized that God was working through his circumstances, and he knew his setbacks were temporary. When you possess a kingdom perspective, you recognize that we are on this earth for a relatively short time, and we recognize that life is short.

With this kingdom perspective, we realize our time and influence on this earth is short. Our actions are more intentional, and we waste less time on the things that are frivolous. We are less indifferent toward humanity. Our motivations are properly aligned with God's. When we view things eternally, we realize and recognize that our pain, loss, and failure are temporary.

Equally, we realize that those things we obtain and possess on earth are temporary. Material wealth may bring us temporary satisfaction and a false sense of security, but eternally they are insignificant. We realize that when this life and all of its heartaches ends, we will go to a better place. Just possessing this perspective brings contentment in life.

Joseph recognized the importance of proper perspective. While he respected and obeyed the human authority he was under, he knew God was his ultimate authority. While his brothers betrayed him and seemingly changed the course of his life, he understood that God would lead him to his ultimate destiny. Pray for and work on developing an eternal or kingdom perspective.

Finally, develop and maintain an attitude of gratitude. Focus on what you do have, not on what you do not have. Each day take a few minutes and thank God for the blessings he has given you. Also, I would encourage you to read the book of Ecclesiastes in the Old Testament. In this book, Solomon reflects on his quest for happiness. He details how he tried and experienced everything. Financial wealth, material wealth, concubines, anything man could buy, he bought. However, in the end, he realized that these things could not bring him happiness. Become content and you will find success, fulfillment, and purpose.

Attribute IV

Proper Motivation/Priorities

Genesis 39:9-10 *"No one is greater in this house than I am. My master has withheld nothing from me except you, because you are his wife. How then could I do such a wicked thing and sin against God?"*

In these verses of Genesis, Joseph reminds Potiphar's wife that he owes his allegiance not only to Potiphar, but to God. Not only would Joseph have sinned against Potiphar, but more importantly, he would have sinned against God. It is apparent Joseph had his priorities aligned. By recognizing the importance of his obedience to God, he was also obedient to his earthly master. I believe Joseph's priorities were like this:

- God and his purpose.
- His family.
- Ministering to humanity.

What Drives You?

The last few years, I have come to realize that I really enjoy encouraging, empowering, and equipping others. I did not discover this passion until I was asked to be a mentor for new sales reps that joined our company a few years ago. I discovered that I really gained a lot of gratification from teaching these ambitious, intelligent young people about selling financial services. I enjoyed explaining the nuances of the banking industry and how to work through the normal rejections associated with selling.

I also came to the realization that this was exactly why I was in sales. I extract a tremendous amount of satisfaction from improving a client's processes, efficiencies, and bottom line profits. When I see a happy customer, it is almost euphoric to me. So, I am constantly seeking skills that make me more effective at this. I have come to understand my drives, my motivations, and my priorities. I work to make other people's lives better and to make my life and my family's life better.

I remember one of my college professors telling us in a strategic planning class that he hoped one day we would have the opportunity to work because we loved the work, and not because we had to work. He went on to explain that he did not teach because he needed the money anymore. He had been very successful and could have retired several years earlier, however, he loved to teach and gained great satisfaction and fulfillment from teaching. This is why prioritizing and assessing our motivations are so important.

Why do you want to succeed? What drives your ambitions? To work toward true success, fulfillment, and purpose, we must constantly evaluate our motivations and priorities. They tend to change over time as we go through various seasons of life and for various reasons.

When we graduate school, we want to make our mark in the workplace. When we get married, we may want to buy a house. When we have children, we spend the next eighteen years preparing and saving so we can send them to school. So, as our life situations change, we need to constantly evaluate our motivations and ensure they still line up with God's purpose for our lives.

I have known people who wanted to achieve a level of authority because they like having power over people. I have known people who wanted to succeed because they wanted to achieve certain financial objectives. I have known some people who wanted to succeed so they could prove to someone that they were capable of success. None of these drivers are necessarily bad. However, to achieve the complete success and fulfillment that Joseph experienced, and that God wants to experience, we need to make sure we have the proper drives and motivations.

While Joseph may have possessed normal ordinary motivations and desires, such as family, love, material success, etc., I
believe that, ultimately, Joseph's main motivation and priority
was to glorify God in all that he did. Once again, it is evident
from scripture that God was with Joseph, and people recognized
it. I sense that Joseph, as should we, reflected on his motivations
often and worked to ensure they were in line with God's purpose.

It is very normal and healthy to have lofty ambitions and
goals. The ability and opportunity to succeed is one of the greatest
things about this country. I think the key is keeping God and his
purpose in those ambitions. For example, when I was younger, I
would often dream of the day that I would make $100K a year. I
would visualize all that I could do if only I could make that kind
of money. At that point in my life, those thoughts never included
giving more to my church, or the ability to send someone on a
mission trip, or making a donation to a children's hospital.
Having the ability to support God's work was not part of my
ultimate motivation.

Truth is, thankfully, by the time I even got close to making
that kind of money, I had experienced some spiritual maturity and
realized the more I am blessed materially, the more responsibility
I have to advance God's kingdom in every way possible. One
thing there will never be a shortage of is needs. You need only
look around you to see opportunities to help others and advance
God's kingdom. We need to make sure that advancing God's
kingdom, which in turn is glorifying him, is an integral foundation of our motivations.

There is nothing wrong with material motivations as long as
we have our priorities in line. If you work hard, sacrifice, save,
you should absolutely be able to travel, shop, and develop hobbies
and interests, whatever it is you enjoy doing. As long as we keep
God's purpose in the forefront and make him a part of our
motivation.

Joseph would not have achieved the level of success he
experienced had he not been motivated. He could have just as
easily been an average servant in Potiphar's house and worked
just hard enough to earn food and shelter for the rest of his life.
When he was thrown in prison, he could have withdrawn and
languished until he died. But Joseph was motivated to glorify

God, and he realized the way for him to achieve that was adhere to the attributes and keep God the primary focus of his motivation.

It is never implied in Genesis that Joseph's drive for success was fueled by the betrayal of his brothers. Although he would eventually end up saving them, revenge was not his motivation. It is never suggested that Joseph succeeded because he aspired to be the second in command of Egypt. Ironically, scripture never suggests that Joseph sought positions of high authority. He just did his job, and things seemed to fall into place. I think one of the most salient points in the story of Joseph and the success he experienced was that his motivations were pure. He simply did what needed to be done to glorify and serve God. For most of Joseph's story, he was not married and did not have children. He was separated from his family and was really alone, so his focus and motivation was simply to live a Godly life. Evaluate your motivations. If you seek success for the wrong reasons, your quest will remain an exercise in futility.

Priorities

Joseph seemed to understand that he needed to focus on fulfilling God's purpose in his life before focusing on any other pursuit. Joseph was an ordinary young man; he surely experienced the same drives and attractions that young adolescent men experience today. However, Joseph kept his priorities in order to achieve great things. After being anointed to second in command behind Pharaoh, Joseph focused on one priority: storing up food and grain during the time of plenty so there would be no shortages when the famine occurred. Joseph seemed to understand that romance, marriage, and family would fall into place in their anointed time. God would set those life events in place in their proper time.

Our priorities change over time and as we mature in life. My priorities today are much different than they were when I was twenty-five. We should constantly re-evaluate our priorities, write them down, refine them, and constantly review them to insure we are adhering to fulfilling these priorities. I examine my priorities from time to time. Based on where I am in life, I can say my priorities are as follows:

- To advance God's Kingdom through financial giving, service, and by being an example to others.
- To provide a financially stable, secure, loving, and supportive home to my family.
- To devote my full and undivided attention to my wife and our marriage.
- To enhance and enrich relationships with family, friends, and others through encouragement, kindness, and respect.
- To enrich my life by learning new skills, accomplishing life goals, and excelling at new hobbies and interests.

Write down your priorities. There is something about writing down goals, priorities, and intentions. It is a large step toward the fulfillment of these endeavors. Pray that your priorities are in line with God's. I truly believe this is one of the many reasons Joseph experienced so much success.

Attribute V

Likability

Genesis 40:6-7 *When Joseph came to them the next morning, he saw that they were dejected. So he asked Pharaoh's officials who were in custody with him in his master's house, why are your faces so sad today?*

It is apparent that Joseph was liked by those in his circle of influence. I visualize Joseph as being a calm, quite, positive, fun, caring person. Because of Joseph's calming and soothing nature, people gravitated to him. Take a moment and think of the people you like. What qualities do they exhibit that make you like them? Sure, we all love someone who is funny or fun to be around at times. However, there are times we like and need those who will encourage us, console us, strengthen us, and re-invigorate us.

Likability is critical for true success, fulfillment, and purpose. Likability is not about charisma or charm. Being likable is not about being the life of the party or telling the funniest jokes. When I speak of likability, I am referring to the kind of person that you like to see coming down the street. The kind of person you enjoy talking to. It is apparent that Joseph was a very likable person. Additionally, it is evident that he could communicate with anyone regardless of their social status, authority, or class. I am not suggesting you have to go through a personality change to be likable. We know there are introverts and extroverts, type A and type B personalities. While we may not be able to change the core of personality, I do think we can change certain aspects of our personalities by changing certain traits in our personality.

In these verses, Joseph has been sent to prison for a crime he did not commit, however, he was sincerely more concerned about the well being of those around him than himself. When people genuinely care about you, you will appreciate their kindness and be drawn to them. His concern and compassion for those he was around was what made Joseph likable.

Genesis indicates that Joseph was Jacob's favorite son. The Bible indicates that Jacob especially loved Joseph because he was one of two sons with his wife Rachel. But Genesis does not indicate that Jacob loved both of his sons with Rachel the most, but specifically Joseph. I believe one of the many reasons Jacob was so drawn to Joseph was Joseph's innocent likability.

When I think of Joseph and what his personality may have been like, I am reminded of a gentleman I worked with for several years at a bank in Nashville. I will not mention his name because he is so humble he would be embarrassed. I am certain this guy was very much like Joseph. He was always happy, and he was always smiling. When he asked you how you were doing, you knew that he really wanted to know how you were doing. We all knew he was a Christian, but he never really brought it up in the workplace unless the timing or situation was just right. He never spoke negatively about anyone, never participated in the latest office gossip, and never told off color or rude jokes. Although he was very intelligent and successful, he did not possess a condescending or arrogant attitude. He was trustworthy, and you could count on him to do what he said he would do. Because of all these things, he was likable. His faith and his passion for God were so strong, you could sense it. If you shared a personal struggle with him, you knew no one else would be told, and you knew he would pray for you. In my mind, he was, and still is, like Joseph. He exhibited the attributes of Joseph.

Additionally, I am confident Joseph was a positive person. I do not think he could have survived the adversity in his life had he been a cynic or pessimist. It is apparent that he dusted off the daily disappointments and setbacks of life and embraced every day with an unshakable, positive attitude. People hate to be around negative people. People are drawn to and magnetized to positive people. Constant negativity is a drag on productivity and success. I believe negative thinking is purely a habit, and as such, is easy to overcome. However, it takes a conscious effort to change any habit.

I also worked with a very negative gentleman for several years. He was a great guy and did very well at his job. However, he was one of the most negative people I have ever met. A group of four of us could go to a restaurant for dinner. Three out of the four could agree it was good, but you could always count on him to say his food was horrible, the service was horrible, or something was horrible about the experience. I came to believe that he possessed such a negative attitude that even if the food or service was great, he had pre-conditioned his mind to think it was bad, and as such, it was.

A few years ago, a well-known entertainer put on a free concert in the Nashville area one beautiful spring Saturday evening. My wife and I attended the show and had a great time. The band did experience some sound issues at the very beginning of the set, but got it corrected, and they put on a great show nonetheless. Everyone around us had a great time. I spoke to this friend of mine the next week and mentioned that we had attended the concert. He told me that he and his wife had also attended the show and it was the worst concert he had ever attended. He went on a tirade about how the sound was horrible, people kept walking in front of him and his wife and blocking their view, and he emphatically stated he would never go back to the venue again. It was the same event we attended, the same band we heard, the same show we saw in the same setting, but we came away with two very different perspectives of the event.

Negative things will and do happen, however, I think our perception of events, and how serious we take things, determine how we react. Constantly being negative, cynical, and pessimistic is not indicative of a person who has the God of the universe walking with them. We need to be diligent in projecting a positive, upbeat, can-do attitude in the workplace and with our family and friends.

Also, smile at people. It makes them wonder what you are up to. Most people love to see a smiling face. Those that do not like to see a smiling face may wonder what you have that they do not have. Ask people how they are doing, and then listen to them. Look people in the eyes; let them know you have a sincere, earnest interest in what is going on in their life. Someone could be facing a situation that you have already overcome. A word of encouragement or sharing how you dealt with a challenge could be just what they need to persevere.

It is easy to let the daily barrage of negative news, problems, and challenges get us down. One of the most powerful testimonies of a faithful person is that they are happy. I am not referring to a phony, superficial happiness, but rather a sincere happiness that we should feel if we are in harmony and in tune with God. If God is for us, then truly no one can be against us. We have the creator and the designer of the universe on our side. Joseph recognized this and chose to be thankful and grateful for the circumstances in his life.

Be thankful and grateful. For the overwhelming majority of us, we are blessed beyond compare. If we can walk, talk, see, and hear, we should be thankful. If we have a healthy family and a roof over our head, we should be exuberant. There are literally millions of people all over the world who truly do not know where their next meal will come from. We live in a country with tremendous opportunities, and we have freedoms that millions of people would literally die and give anything to have. We should be happy. When we are genuinely happy, people will be drawn to us.

Joseph chose to be happy wherever he was. He understood that he was blessed with God-given skills and abilities, and he was confident that in God's time, he would be able to harness and use those skills for God's purpose. Pray for a better attitude. Make a conscious effort to be nice to people. You will be amazed at the response.

I remember when our daughter was in college, she worked at a local drug store during the summers in between semesters. She told my wife and me that one of our senior pastors from the local church came in to the drug store on a regular basis and she was amazed at how rude he was to the cashiers in the drug store. I was floored to think a reputable leader in a local church would act that way. I am sure he meant nothing by it and was probably consumed by a thousand other thoughts as he made his way through that drug store. But people know us, and people watch us. We all have bad days, and there will inevitably be times when we will not be jovial or happy. However, as Christians, we must always be diligent not to be rude or inconsiderate to others.

Watch people's body language. Do they appear to be despondent or in despair? We should emulate Joseph's actions with the two inmates in the prison, ask them how they are, and if nothing else, tell them you will pray for them. Offering an encouraging word to someone who is going through a difficult situation could be the very thing they need to get them through a burdensome time. It is so easy to be consumed with our own problems. Reflect on past challenges and opportunities in your life and how you responded to them. Share with others the mistakes you made and the opportunities you seized. People often appreciate the insight from someone who has been through a similar situation.

Likable people are more likely to be successful. If people like you, they will gravitate toward you, listen to your opinions, and look to you for advice. They will come to you for guidance and assistance if you try to be sincerely likable. The easiest way to be likable is to be positive, upbeat, and transparent. More importantly, people are more likely to help you achieve success if they like you.

Additionally, I like people who are courteous and respectful toward others. If someone opens a door for you or lets you go first in the checkout at the supermarket, thank them. If someone lets you have the parking spot that they were going to pull into, thank them. Likewise, make an effort to let others pass before you, hold the door open for them, or give them the parking spot; you may just brighten their day. I sadly sense that manners and chivalry are a thing of the past. Just when I am convinced of that, someone will prove me wrong. I really appreciate and respect young people who refer to men as sir and women as ma'am. By practicing these simple manners, you will leave lasting impressions on others.

Joseph observed the countenance of others and took notice if something seemed amiss. This is why he asked the baker and wine taster what was bothering them. Joseph possessed the ability and interest in making others feel special. One of the easiest ways to make people like you is to express interest in them and to make them feel special.

Starting in May of 2007, I had the opportunity to attend a three year graduate banking school on the campus of Louisiana

State University in Baton Rouge. The program is one of the most respected banking schools in the country and is well known for its well-rounded, grueling curriculum. Approximately six hundred bankers converge on the campus every May and spend two weeks in numerous classes, projects, and assignments. Then, each student is required to complete several home projects throughout the year until class resumes again. The third and final year culminates with the students running a simulation bank model over the course of several financial quarters. It was an honor and a challenge to join the ranks of fellow bankers who have had the privilege of attending.

During our freshman year, we had to take a class on strategy that was taught by a banker named George Schloegel. George was in his seventies, but full of life and vitality. He had started working for a bank in South Mississippi in the sixties and had been very successful. He rose through the ranks and had served as CEO for many years. This bank is now one of the most well-respected, best performing banks in the country. During this class, George went around the room and asked everyone to identify themselves, tell the class where they lived, what bank they worked for, and then to tell the class something unique and interesting about themselves. When it was my turn, I identified myself, told the class where I lived, and the name of the bank I was with. I told the class and Mr. Schloegel that I loved music, had played piano since I was a child, and performed with a country band for ten years or so when I was younger.

A couple of months after I returned home, I received a hand-written card in the mail from George Schloegel. He thanked me for my participation in the class, and he noted that he would like to hear some of my music at some point and wished me the best. Not only was I blown away that this important executive from a large bank in Mississippi took the time to write me a note, but I was amazed that he remembered everything I told about myself in class that day. When I returned the next year, I asked some of my classmates if they had received a similar card, and they all had received one just as I did. As I thought about this, it dawned on me, this was one of the many reasons George Schloegel was so well liked. He possessed the ability to make people feel special and important. I have no doubt that this ability is one of the many reasons George has been so successful. People like to feel special. Taking a few minutes to recognize something about someone will make people like you.

Humility

It is crucial that we possess a spirit of humility in our lives. People will gravitate toward us and turn to us if we possess humbleness. Surely you have known someone who bragged or boasted about their accomplishments and achievements all of the time? It is extremely hard to like someone who is prideful and brags all of the time. Sure, we all want to brag on our kids for being a good athlete or for being a good student. However, we need to evaluate our behavior and make sure we are humble regarding any and all blessings in our lives.

I have had the privilege of working with some of the most successful bankers in the southeast throughout my career. These men and women have led some of the most successful financial institutions through recessions and expansions. They have contributed to increased stakeholder value in their organizations, and provided jobs and security for people in the communities. However, I can truly say that the vast majority of them are very humble people. They understand and recognize that their success is not simply a result of their efforts and abilities. They recognize that they would not be where they are if it were not for other people who believed in them, trusted them, and gave them opportunities. The most successful people and the most likable people are those who give the credit for their success to God and to others. No one likes a sore loser. No one likes a sore winner either. Be gracious in defeat and be gracious in victory.

Approachability

We need to convey a sense of approachability to others. Observe your body language and facial expressions to insure you are inviting others into your space. Think of a time you have wanted to approach someone and you saw that they appeared angry or upset or un-interested. You probably walked away without bothering them. If we want to reach others, we need to let them know they can approach us.

Through the years, I have visited countless community banks. In some of those banks, the CEO or president had offices on the ground floor where everyone who walked by could see them, approach them, and talk to them. Many of those bankers have told me that they experience a lot of distractions throughout the day. They have to shake hands with everyone that walks by, they have to stop what they are doing and talk to the farmers about the weather or their crops, or they have to look at pictures of the most recent grandbaby. As distracting as it may be, these bankers tell me they would not have it any other way. They want their customers and other bank employees to know they are accessible if needed. On the other hand, I have visited banks where the CEO or president had their office on the second, third, or fourth floor of the bank where very few people could distract or approach them. In my honest opinion, I fear that this sends a message to customers and to other employees that the executive is too busy or is not interested in those daily interactions and distractions. I am not saying one is right and the other is wrong. I just wonder if the executive with the office away from everyone else is missing out on opportunities to bond with other employees or clients.

Regardless, make a conscious effort to be accessible, approachable, and greet others with an inviting smile, hand shake, or embrace. People will gravitate to you and want to interact with you. More importantly, it could create an opportunity to minister to someone in a time of need.

Religious, Political, Moral Discussions

Ancient Egypt had its own religious beliefs, customs, and Gods. It is very likely that Potiphar practiced one of those religions. However, according to Genesis, Potiphar saw that "God was with Joseph." How did Potiphar know that God was with Joseph? I believe he recognized something very different in Joseph's demeanor and his countenance. He recognized his dependability, his trustworthiness, his contentment, and his honor. Potiphar, the captain of the prison guard, even the Pharaoh saw something in

Joseph apparently lacking in most others. For some reason, his behavior was consistent, constant, different, and respectable. He was an anomaly among the others.

It is no secret that secular or non-Christians often view Christians very negatively. Why is that the case? Well, perhaps there is a humanistic innate disdain toward believers. While I do believe there is an instinctual hate or malice toward believers, I think there could be more to this negative perception of Christians. Sometimes we Christians tend to have a chip on our shoulder. We tend to have an arrogant or condescending attitude toward the behavior of others. We must be very careful not to display or possess this type of attitude toward others. I am convinced that Joseph was respectful toward his Egyptian co-workers even though his beliefs differed from the Egyptians greatly.

Moral and political issues can be very divisive. You only have to look at how polarized our society has become politically to sense the differences in political opinions. Discussing these matters can be very polarizing. I think Christians have to be very careful and not appear confrontational when discussing political issues. I am not suggesting we should remain silent and allow our rights to be absolved. What I am saying is Christians should be very intentional when discussing certain issues. Like Joseph, we must think before we speak and remember that every word renders a reaction, either positive or negative. Genesis never mentions anything about Joseph being divisive or difficult in this foreign land he was in. Perhaps it was his personality, or perhaps, because of his mature faith, he realized he could touch more people for God and accomplish more for God by being obedient, dependable, trust-worthy, and kind. He chose to display his faith in his God through kind and dependable action, not through polarizing discussions regarding the hot political topics of the day.

I do not believe for a moment that Joseph walked around Potiphar's house condemning the Egyptians for worshipping a pagan God. I do not suspect he sat around the table at lunch telling the Egyptians they were going to Hell if they did not change their ways. When I visualize Joseph's demeanor, I picture him as a gentle, kind, loving, non-adversarial, and forgiving person. I sense he left the judging and condemnation to God. Once again, I am not saying we should abandon or bury our beliefs in public; however, we need to be more like Joseph. In my opinion, this is why the author of Genesis pointed out three different times that Joseph's superlatives recognized that "God was with Joseph." It was obvious in his behavior, it was obvious in the way he handled himself around others, and it was obvious in his work.

One thing is for certain; Joseph stood out among his Egyptian peers. Whatever he did, or did not do, it was very obvious that he was different, and different in a good way. We should constantly be diligent and cautious regarding what we discuss in our given surroundings. We should be an anomaly as Joseph was.

Years ago, my wife and I were in a small Sunday school class in East Tennessee, composed of other young couples. We had a visitor one Sunday morning. He was alone, very shy, and it was obvious he was not comfortable in a church setting. Somewhere in the discussion that morning the topic of abortion came up. Several members of the class became very vocal about abortion and began discussing the graphic details of the various procedures. Suddenly, the visitor started sobbing, got up, and walked right out of the class and left. He never came back again. We never knew what happened or what kind of pain we had rekindled during that discussion. It was very apparent that this was an emotional issue for this guy. The point is this; it is very easy to become emotional regarding moral beliefs. Nothing riles tempers like these types of discussions. As believers, we need to be very cautious in discussing these issues because we never know who may be listening. I want people to think I am different. I want to stand out in a crowd. I want others to see the difference God has made in my life. However, I want them to think that for the right reasons. Our main mission as Christians is to reach others and to love others. We do that through love, kindness, and by sharing the grace that has been poured upon us so generously.

In trying to get others to like us, remember this. It is important that others like us. It is paramount to our success that others like us, embrace us, promote us, and throw their support behind us. However, sometimes there are going to be some people who just do not like us. I really struggle with this because I want everyone to like me. However, there have been people I have met who, for whatever reason, did not like me. As painful as that may be, I have to accept it. Maybe it's just a personality conflict. Perhaps it is for some other reason. But in the end, I have to accept it and respect it. We cannot force someone to like us. Likewise, we cannot buy someone's affection. We should be who we are and make every effort to like others and to have them like us, but in the end, we have to accept that some may not like us. We cannot dwell on it or obsess over it, just accept it, and keep being nice. We may never know the basis for this dislike. It could be jealousy, envy, whatever. But we will meet some who do not like us.

In the end, if we treat others the way we want to be treated, for the most part, others will gravitate to us and like us. Joseph liked others and Joseph respected others, and many liked him and respected him. He certainly encountered people who did not like him, but he did not let them distract or de-rail his destiny with success.

Attribute VI

Strategic/Critical Thinking

Genesis 41:33-38 *And Joseph said "Now let Pharaoh look for a discerning and wise man and put him in charge of the land of Egypt. Let Pharaoh appoint commissioners over the land to take a fifth of the harvest of Egypt during the seven years of abundance. They should collect all the food of these good years that are coming and store up the grain under the authority of Pharaoh, to be kept in the cities for food. This food should be held in reserve for the country, to be used during the seven years of famine that will come upon Egypt, so that the country may not be ruined by the famine." The plan seemed good to Pharaoh and to all his officials. So Pharaoh asked them, "Can we find anyone like this man, one in whom is the spirit of God?"*

When God does ultimately reward us with responsibility, how do we respond? When Pharaoh placed Joseph second in command, he was prepared to act. Joseph was not frozen by indecisiveness. He sprang into immediate, intentional action. It is evident that he had prepared himself mentally for the challenges that lay ahead. When opportunities or obstacles arise, we must be ready to act wisely and strategically. I have known so many people through the years that when faced with a tough decision, their best action was inaction. We used to call it "paralysis by analysis." So many of us are afraid to take action because we fear it will be the wrong action.

We certainly do not want to rush into a decision without giving thought to the ensuing consequences. However, it is also our responsibility to think strategically, critically, and definitively. If we act, there is the chance we fail. If we do not act, we have already failed. Joseph understood how critical it was that Egypt immediately begin storing up grain while the harvest was plentiful.

The best definition for strategic/critical thinking is this; it is the unique critical ability to identify and pursue future opportunities while managing the daily challenges; the ability to keep a sharp focus on the long-term goals of a person, company, government (as in Joseph's case) without deviating or being distracted by temporary or short-term obstacles. Opportunities, challenges, initiatives, and drives constantly change. We must possess the intuitiveness, nimbleness, and agility to recognize the changes, identify opportunities, adapt to our current environment, and react quickly.

Joseph's skill sets expanded from being a shepherd or herder to becoming the head of the servants for Potiphar. After a period of time in prison, he ascended to second in command of the prison. After he was released from prison and came to serve the King, he was placed second in command of the largest government in the Middle East at the time. He did not possess the past experiences to perform these duties to his fullest. However, he was apparently very well prepared to take on this role.

Joseph likely arrived in Egypt as a slave around sixteen years of age. Roughly fourteen years later, at the age of thirty, he was second in command of Egypt. Joseph did not have the pedigree of a high ranking official; he possessed no college education or specialized training. However, I think Joseph was constantly preparing for his coming responsibilities. He possessed the wisdom, vision, and strategic/critical thinking skills necessary to achieve the results he knew he had to achieve.

After Joseph interpreted Pharaoh's dreams regarding the drought, and when Pharaoh placed Joseph second in command, he was ready to spring into action. Joseph knew there was only a certain amount of time to prepare for the drought. He was keenly aware of the significance and urgency of a quick response. God opens windows of opportunities for us. Usually these windows are open for only a short period of time. If we are hesitant in taking action, we may miss out on the opportunity all together.

Timing is everything. I have worked in sales for over twenty years and could tell countless stories of both opportunities won and opportunities lost because of nothing more than simple timing. There have been times when I happened to be in the right place at the right time and was able to identify an opportunity and seize it. There have been times when I was too early or too late in an opportunity and missed it.

My marriage is a perfect example of this. I had met my wife through mutual friends probably six years before we ever started dating. Every time I saw her, I was dating someone else, or she was dating someone else. Then, it just so happened we met again in 1992, and neither of us was involved in another relationship. I had always been attracted to her, and something told me not to let the opportunity pass by this time. I sensed that she had the same feeling, and the rest is history.

In 1997, one of my dad's brothers passed away in Myrtle Beach, South Carolina. My father and another uncle of mine really wanted to go to his funeral. When Dad told me about the funeral arrangements, I got to thinking that I should drive them over to South Carolina for the funeral. Initially, I really did not think I needed to miss work, and I had some vacation days planned for later that month.

However, that night something told me I needed to drive my dad and uncle to South Carolina. I had the gnawing sense that I would never get this opportunity again. My wife agreed, and I called my manager and asked her if I could change my vacation dates. My dad and uncle were ecstatic that I offered to drive them over. We had a wonderful time considering the circumstances, and spent some precious time together for a few days.

Less than a year later, my father was diagnosed with stage four cancer and would die less than a year later. If I had not acted on that opportunity, I would have missed out on one of the most meaningful trips of my life. Just recently, the other uncle passed away. At his funeral, I kept thinking of that trip we made to South Carolina, and I was so thankful that I did not let that opportunity pass by.

Be alert for opportunities. Pray for wisdom to act strategically and critically regarding the opportunity. Be ready to act
strategically when an opportunity arises. This is applicable in any
aspect of our lives. I read a lot of books related to improving
communication skills, sales skills, time management improvement, etc. Although I have been in sales for twenty plus years, I
recognize there is always room for improvement in what I do.
Additionally, everything changes. We have to be flexible and less
adverse to change in our lives.

I believe life was designed so that we are always learning
new skills. God wants life to be an adventure. He wants us to
experience that same excitement as adults that we did as children.
Think back to when you were a child; remember how exhilarating
it was to learn new concepts. Read and learn. It will enhance your
value and effectiveness in every aspect of your life. We will
explore this more when we look at adaptability.

Critical Thinking

Critical thinking has been defined as the ability to discern or
evaluate a situation, make a decision about that situation, and
understand the potential benefits and ramifications of that
decision. It also encompasses questioning material presented to
us, and not just taking someone's word at face value. I am not
saying we should be cynical about every idea or issue, but we
should always explore why something is being done.

Finding Your Niche

For several years, I worked, in a sales capacity, for a large
regional bank in the Southeast United States. My team provided
payment solutions to the commercial customers of the bank. Once
or twice a year, we would meet in Orlando, Florida to discuss
initiatives, review best practices, and to swap success stories.
There were approximately thirty folks on the sales team throughout the corporation. As is often the case, about twenty percent of
these folks provided roughly eighty percent of the new business
and revenue.

Invariably, the most successful salespeople on this team had found a niche. They had indentified a specific sector of customers that they seemed to have a connection with. One of the sales executives only targeted large retail box store chains. Granted, he usually only signed one account per year, but that one account dwarfed the hundreds of accounts the other sales people sold throughout the whole year. Additionally, he earned significantly more commissions than the rest of us simply based on the volume these accounts provided.

A lady in Daytona Beach, Florida only focused on the hotel, travel, and entertainment sector. This is a huge source of prospects in the tourist areas of Florida. She had spent several years learning the nuances of the lodging business. She often spoke at lodging conventions about relevant issues and was considered the expert on payment services for the lodging industry. She consistently finished in the top two or three per-formers of our division.

Another guy who happened to be bi-lingual focused mainly on Mexican restaurants. His ability to speak Spanish gave him a distinct advantage on other providers, even when his pricing may not have been the most competitive. Point is we cannot be experts at everything. We need to look for a niche to serve and become an expert at that niche.

When I think of niches, I always think of a hair stylist in the small town I grew up in named Raymond. Raymond had worked in various fields through the years, including sales, before decid-ing to open his salon. There was no shortage of salons, beauty shops, and barber shops in this small town. The interesting thing is Raymond charged at least twice as much as any other hair stylist in town for a haircut. More interesting is that he stayed completely booked up. Often, you would have to set an appoint-ment a month in advance to get in to see him. At the time, I could hardly afford to use him on a regular basis. But on rare occasions, for example, if I had an important job interview, I would schedule an appointment with Raymond. Going to his salon in his home was an experience. The lighting and ambiance was always perfect, he played relaxing, new age music in the background, and always offered a beverage of choice while he styled or cut your hair. You could sip a glass of wine, a bottle of beer, or whatever you wanted during the appointment. He always blocked off an hour of time for your cut. He always spent the entire hour uninterrupted with you. He would chat, give advice, and then give you the best haircut money could buy. It was no secret that Raymond styled the hair for many of the wealthy, affluent, and privileged of Cleveland, Tennessee. However, he treated me, or anyone else, just like he treated those folks. He even charged me the same amount as he charged the wealthy. He made no apologies for his prices. If you did not like his prices, you did not have to come back.

Raymond built an incredible and unique business out of what most considered and perceived to be an ordinary experience. Raymond understood that he could charge more by creating a different experience that was valuable and special to the client. He also understood and knew his niche. He understood that his market was small and that he could not attract everyone in town. But he knew, by creating a value added experience, some people would, and did, pay more for his hair cuts. Raymond was a very intuitive, wise person. He made good money from a common trade because he understood the importance of serving a niche.

Joseph also recognized this principle. He knew he was a leader. Leading others was his niche. He did not attempt to be a farmer and grow grain. He did not attempt to handle the economics or the logistics of growing and storing the food. His niche was identifying the people he needed to use to achieve his goals. Seek and identify your sweet spot. There are needs everywhere. Diligently be looking for that niche to serve. This applies to all walks of our lives, not just professionally. Recognizing a niche and becoming a specialist in that niche will give you a strategic advantage over many others.

Plan Strategically in All You Do

Strategic planning is crucial for any business. In the early 2000s, when the real estate market was hot, many community banks changed directions strategically. There were some banks that had been historically conservative. Due to pressures from investors and board members, they implemented extremely risky lending strategies in pursuit of profits. Had these banks stuck to their conservative lending culture, they would have likely survived the impending recession.

Many experts in the financial services industry had predicted that there would have to be a burst in the real estate bubble at some point. While these banks booked record earnings for a few years, sure enough, in 2007, the real estate market crashed. From 2008 through 2012, 465 banks failed in the United States. The banks that survived the recession were the ones who had stuck to their conservative strategy and who were not lured into over concentration in the risky real estate business.

Preparing for the Famine

One of the most basic economic principles is that economies are cyclical, much like weather patterns. Economies go through periods of expansion, retraction, and recession. Bankers watched the economy grow at a searing pace from about 2002 through 2006. Home values soared, the stock market appreciated to record highs, and everyone seemed to be making money. Stories of banks making "liar" loans, "no-doc" loans, and "subprime" lending were rampant in the industry. Many of us scratched our heads wondering how lenders could have become so reckless. Economists warned that there would be a real estate bubble and that it would eventually burst. Many banks saw the "drought" coming and stuck to a conservative business model. Many bankers remembered the basic precept of risk management, that is, not to put all of your eggs in one basket, and they survived the recession.

Likewise, many consumers continued to spend and spend. They continued to buy larger houses that they truly could not afford. They continued to buy bigger cars, bigger boats, and more things. Borrowers had become confident the rising equity in their homes would keep them "above water." While the economy was still good, they were able to cash flow the debt. However, when a job was lost, or a salary was reduced due to cut hours, the households simply could not sustain.

There will be seasons of plenty and seasons of famine in our lives. All things are cyclical. It is crucial that we maintain proper perspectives as Joseph did. Joseph understood the concept of saving during times of plenty. By saving and preparing, we can survive, or even prosper, during the times of famine. Joseph had the foresight to turn the catastrophe into an opportunity. Not only did he put enough grain back to feed the region during the time of plenty, but he recognized the opportunity to sell the excess grain to other countries, creating a windfall for Egypt while other nations withered under the drought.

Trends and Fads

While on the topic of strategic/critical thinking, never assume that just because everyone else is doing something, that you should be doing it as well. There are countless examples of situations where a majority of people followed a trend or pattern, only to be led off a cliff.

I go back to the banks I discussed above. When the economy was hot, so many of the progressive bankers thought the conservative bankers were narrow-minded and ignorant for not ramping up their commercial real estate lending. Once again, when the recession hit, the conservative banks survived when many of the aggressive banks failed. Seek God's wisdom regarding your strategy. Seek wisdom from folks who are wise and have life experiences, but do not simply follow the crowd.

My Seven Year Famine

Fortunately, my wife and I always planned for a famine. Sensing the impending meltdown of the real estate market, I feared there would be a lot of instability in the banking industry. So we saved when possible, and we tried to keep debt manageable in case either or both of us lost our jobs. I had spent close to twenty years working for two institutions during my career. In the last three years, I have worked for four different companies. I know a lot of people who suffered through this recession because they had not made provisions for a downturn.

Because of strategic/critical thinking, Joseph not only ensured that Egypt and the region would survive the drought, Egypt actually prospered. In his wisdom, Joseph recognized there would be an opportunity for Egypt to feed the entire region. Not only did

Joseph's strategic thinking save Egypt and the countries surrounding them, but Egypt prospered from his strategic planning. This is the kind of success we can experience when we think strategically and critically.

Another term used in the banking industry is known as "asset utilization." This ratio gives an indication of how the assets of a company are being leveraged. The higher the ratio, the more income the company or bank produces. To experience optimum success, we need to calculate and improve our "asset utilization." Are we using the assets we have, materially, spiritually, and vocationally, to achieve God's ultimate purpose? Our employer's ultimate purpose? And our ultimate purpose? We should compile a balance sheet of our assets, not just in financial terms, but interpersonally as well to determine what our assets are, but to make sure we are utilizing these assets to their maximum effectiveness.

Gifts

In speaking of our interpersonal assets, I am referring to our natural gifts. Everyone is wired different, and everyone possesses different gifts and talents. Some possess the gift of leadership abilities; some, the gift of being a good salesperson. Some people are more analytical and make great accountants. Some people are good with their hands and make great carpenters.

I have been successful at sales, but I am not a strong manager or supervisor, and I really do not possess leadership skills. I recognize my strengths, and I work within the confines of my abilities. It would be absurd for me to pursue a CEO position, or CFO position, or to be a carpenter.

Analyze your skills and your passions and then focus your efforts on being successful in that given space. Do not spend years attempting to be something you are not good at and that you will not enjoy. Joseph recognized his skills and capitalized on them. He did not attempt to grow the grain, cut the grain, or count the grain. He obviously placed the proper people with the proper skills in those positions, and he managed the initiative with much success.

We need to look inside ourselves and identify and recognize our gifts, both vocational and spiritual, and be grateful for them. Over the years, I have determined that my vocational gift is selling; not because I am a great salesperson, but because I pick up on details, I listen to clients and customers, and I experience a deep level of satisfaction when I provide a solution to a challenge. My spiritual gift is along those same lines. I like to talk to people, listen to people, and offer encouragement, advice, and wisdom.

Strategic Vision

Opportunities await us at every turn. Just look at the meteoric rise of some companies in the modern tech era in which we live. Mark Zuckerberg, Facebook's founder, recognized the need for social media websites. Bill Gates possessed a vision of a computer operating system that could run the blossoming personal computer industry. There are dozens of examples of people who possess the strategic vision to see an opportunity, although it may be short lived, and seize it.

Delegating

Many of us are control freaks. We feel that nothing will be done correctly if we cannot do it ourselves. This is a very inhibiting practice that we must correct to be successful. If we struggle with delegating responsibility, we must learn to overcome it. We cannot devote our efforts to the things we are good at if we are hovering over everyone we work with and trying to have a hand in every task we encounter.

We must delegate tasks and responsibilities when appropriate to those whom we trust will get these tasks completed. As a salesperson, I need to spend the vast majority of my time cultivating leads, presenting proposals, leading the sales cycle, following up on proposals, and marketing to new prospects. If I spend ninety percent of my time "hand holding" routine customer service issues, I will not achieve my goals. This has always been a challenge for me as I feel I have to see an incident through to its resolution. I am not achieving my objectives when I do this.

I observe so many people, in variable walks of life, being dragged down by refusing to delegate. In all honesty, I would say that the reluctance to delegate is the Achilles heel of many professionals. We need to hand these responsibilities off to those who are responsible for them and assertively assume they will be resolved.

I can only assume that Joseph focused on what he needed to focus on. Joseph possessed the wisdom to recognize the value of his time and efforts, and he knew where he needed to focus his energies. Joseph was facing a window of opportunity to gather before a cataclysmic drought engulfed Egypt. He could not afford to be distracted by mundane and routine tasks. He possessed that enviable trait of recognizing what needed to be delegated. This was a key reason he was so successful.

I can promise you this, if you will honestly evaluate how your time is being spent, you will identify opportunities to delegate and hand off certain tasks that rob you of precious time that should be spent on accomplishing your higher desires. This can be true in our personal lives as well as our professional lives. You cannot, and should not, volunteer, or be volunteered, for responsibilities that distract you from your ultimate goals. This applies to Church, civic groups, fantasy football leagues, etc.

All Actions Have Consequences

Never forget that our actions have lasting consequences. Small, subtle decisions made today can lead to life-altering decisions later. In the 1980s, my father owned a used car business in east Tennessee. There was a young man just a couple of years older than me who worked for my dad and several of the other dealers around town at various times. I came to know him and really liked him. He was a bright, likable, young man with a young wife and a couple of beautiful children. He had a great personality, and everyone assumed he had a bright future ahead of him.

As fate would have it, I did not see him for several years. Then late in the summer of 1990, I happened to run into him at a gas station one evening. He was with an older woman. I noticed immediately that his personality and demeanor had changed drastically. He had lost a lot of weight, his eyes seemed bloodshot and glassy, and he appeared jittery and nervous. I asked him about his wife and family, and he indicated that he and his wife had been separated for some time, and he was seeing this older lady.

Later I mentioned to my dad that I had ran into this guy, and Dad indicated that he had heard the guy had gotten on drugs, lost his family, and was spiraling downhill fast. Just before Christmas in December of 1990, I was watching the local news one morning, and the anchor reported there had been a murder of a woman in our hometown, and the police were searching for a suspect. I glanced at the composite drawing of the suspect and thought the sketch looked like someone I knew, but I could not place the face. A couple of days later, they arrested this guy and charged him with murder of the lady he had been with that evening a few months before.

As it turned out, he had beaten her to death in a drug fueled rage because she would not give him money to buy drugs. He later pled guilty to second degree murder and is still in prison today for the crime. By now, his children are grown, her children are grown, and each of these children, both his and hers, have had to grow up without a parent in their lives. Small decisions that seemed insignificant at the time ultimately led both of these people to life-altering points. His, to live most of life in prison deprived of seeing his children grow up, and her, murdered and gone, never to see her children grow up.

I can say with probable certainty that this guy never thought he would end up in this predicament. Like so many others, when he first started using drugs, he probably thought he would never become the addict. I know this is an extreme example, but it happens every day. What may seem benign at the time, like a decision to drink and drive, a decision to try drugs, a decision to accept a Facebook invitation from an old flame you have not seen in years, a decision to cut corners on a project, or a decision to fudge on an expense report, can lead us down very destructive paths. Think strategically, think of everything that is at risk, and never forget that every action has consequences.

Attribute VII

Stewardship

Genesis 41:47-49 *During the seven years of abundance the land produced plentifully, Joseph collected all the food produced in those seven years of abundance in Egypt and stored it in the cities. In each city he put the food grown in the fields surrounding it. Joseph stored up huge quantities of grain, like the sand of the sea; it was so much that he stopped keeping records because it was beyond measure.*

When we think of stewardship, we generally think about tithing or giving money. Certainly, stewardship includes tithing and our responsibility to give back to God. However, true stewardship encompasses so much more. We are expected to be good stewards of our money, our time, our employer's resources, our health, and our efforts. The list can go on and on. Developing a true stewardship attitude can enrich our lives, as well as those we touch.

Financial Stewardship

Stress created from financial problems is one of the leading causes of divorce in our country. Financial problems can lead to many other problems, including health issues, and even alcohol and drug abuse. To experience true success, fulfillment, and purpose, it is crucial that we be good stewards of our finances. Achieving financial freedom can be an exhilarating experience; sadly, so many Americans never have the opportunity to know this feeling. Joseph obviously understood the concept of steward-ship.

In my many years of banking, I have encountered countless cases of poor financial stewardship and responsibility. Interest-ingly, in talking with folks who were having financial problems, they always thought it was an income issue. If they could only make more money, they could get on their feet. However, in looking at their financial situation, the problem usually turned out to be an expense control issue. If you have spending issues, you can never generate enough income to cover the expense problem.

If you are not doing so, I encourage you to start a budget and adhere to it, just like businesses do. I have never worked for a company who did not create a budget and track their income and expenses during a period of time to insure they were on track with the financial plan. If expenses exceeded budgeted expenses, they wanted to identify why and take the necessary steps to correct the expense problem. If revenues were falling short of projections, they wanted to know why and what needed to be done to increase revenues. Households should do the same. I encourage you to treat your personal finances just like it is a business. Create a budget and track your expenses and revenue monthly, quarterly, and annually. In most cases, people are amazed at the frivolous spending that goes on when expenses are not tracked or moni-tored.

Just observing, monitoring, and being aware of where your money is going will cause you to stop and think before you spend on something you may not need. Oftentimes, we cannot immed-iately influence our income, but we can influence where the money is going. I encourage you to look for some budgeting tools on the internet. There are many that are free to use, so if you are having financial challenges, start taking control of your finances.

Additionally, I have been amazed at how many couples do not discuss financial goals or financial problems. Their salaries simply go into the bank account while the mortgage, car payment, credit card payments, and utility bills go out of the account, and this goes on month after month, year after year. The reason couples avoid discussing financial matters is because it can become very emotional and often lead to finger-pointing and blaming each other for the problems. This is not the way to approach discussing financial matters. These discussions should be handled in a civil, positive, constructive manner. I have known people who hide spending from their spouses. This is very dangerous and potentially toxic to the relationship. Financial issues need to be kept transparent and need to be discussed often.

Achieving financial independence opens additional doors of opportunity. When you have manageable debt and savings, you can take some chances on potential opportunities. Let me give you some examples of this. In 2000, my wife and I had just relocated to Nashville where I had accepted a new job. During this time, a lot of "start up" banks where opening in the southeast. I was approached by some co-workers who were going to invest in a "start up" bank. The initial investment would be valued at one dollar per share, but there was a minimum of 100,000 share purchase, or $100K to get in on the opportunity. There was no guaranty the venture would be a success. The investors were fully aware that they could easily lose all of their investment, or they may possibly see a windfall profit from the opportunity. At the time, our daughter was just starting high school, and we had just built a new house. We were working hard on building our daughter's college fund. I discussed it with my wife, and we just did not feel we were in a place at that time to take that kind of gamble. It would have taken all of our savings and our daughter's college fund and then some to get into the "start up," so I graciously passed on the opportunity.

The company opened, and although they did experience some hiccups along the way, including a mild recession in late 2001 and 2002 that delayed the execution of their initial business plan, the company eventually went public in 2005. The stock opened on the NASDAQ exchange at $10.00 per share, essentially earning the initial investors a 10 times return on their initial investment. Some of the guys I worked with that had invested were understandably jubilant over their windfall. I was happy for them, but I was somewhat sad that I had missed out on the opportunity. If the timing had been somewhat different, I could have participated in this wonderful opportunity and reaped the benefits from it.

As I discussed in the strategic thinking chapter, timing is crucial. A few years later a group of businessmen in Kentucky were hoping to form a "start up" bank. The minimum to invest was significantly lower than the example above, so I did invest in this one at a much lower amount. By this time, there was a lot of concern and chatter in the industry about an impending real estate bubble and resulting recession. Investors were beginning to have second thoughts about buying into "start up" banks. The organizers of this bank were not able to raise the required capital mandated by the Federal Deposit Insurance Corporation, or FDIC, and the deal fell apart. Fortunately, my investment was returned in full. Point being, I had missed an incredible opportunity earlier because I was not prepared financially. By the time I was prepared financially, this window of opportunity for this type of investment had passed, at least for the foreseeable future.

On the topic of timing, the bank that went public at $10.00 a share did very well for a few years. Some of the initial investors kept buying more stock in the bank, anticipating it would continue to ascend in value. When the recession hit in 2008, this bank took some substantial losses in the commercial real estate market and eventually failed. Those who had cashed out when the bank went public did very well. Unfortunately, those who invested more, or did not cash out their initial investment, would eventually lose everything on the bank.

A few months ago, I saw a very interesting interview with Dolly Parton. Dolly is one of the most successful country music songwriters/singers in the business, and she is also an extremely savvy business person. She told the interviewer that back in the 1970s, she was approached by Elvis Presley, who wanted to cut a version of her hit song "*I Will Always Love You*." Dolly had taken the song to the top of the country charts in the early seventies. She said she was ecstatic that Elvis wanted to record a version of the song, and a meeting was set in Nashville for him to record the song. Shortly before the meeting, she said she received a call from Elvis' manager, Colonel Tom Parker. In this phone call, Colonel Parker explained to her that in order for Elvis to cut the song, she would have to sign over 50% of the songwriting royalties to him. In the interview, she said she was very conflicted. Certainly she wanted Elvis to record the song, but she was extremely reluctant to sign over the residual royalty rights to this song she wrote. In the end, she told Mr. Parker that she would not sign over the royalties, and the deal fell through.

In 1993, Whitney Houston recorded the song for the movie soundtrack to "*The Bodyguard*," and the song went on to sell millions of copies, earning Dolly significant royalties. She told the interviewer, and I am paraphrasing, "When I recorded and released '*I Will Always Love You*,' I laughed all the way to the bank. When Whitney recorded and released the song, I bought the bank!"

The point of this story is this. Dolly was in a good position financially, so she did not have to give away the royalties of the song to Elvis Presley. Because she was prepared financially at that time, she could pass on this opportunity and wait until a better opportunity came along. When you gain financial freedom, you are poised to make better financial decisions at the right time. You are not desperate and can weigh all the ramifications of a financial decision with much more clarity.

Certainly we should save and improvise for those famines in our lives. Sometimes, however, no amount of saving or planning can prepare us for unexpected or unanticipated catastrophic events that happen in our lives. Natural disasters, severe recessions, extended periods of time between jobs, severe health issues, and sometimes a business opportunity that did not work out can decimate our financial resources.

When these events happen, they are not necessarily indications of failure or disobedience on our part. Sometimes bad things just happen. All we can do is the best we can do. The point of this section is this. Save and plan for potential "famines." However, do not become obsessed with hoarding money, assets, or resources. When this happens, we are turning our belongings into a God. Ultimately, we will find out that we cannot place our confidence in things that rot and rust and become worthless.

We are the stewards over everything and anything that God puts in our hands. That includes our time, our relationships, and our financial resources. It is very evident that Joseph understood the concept of stewardship.

If we are good stewards of our financial resources, we are free and empowered to do so much more in life. Practicing sound biblical financial principles can help us achieve and work toward financial freedom. Using common sense about money, debt, and investing will help us achieve our financial goals. Using budgets, tracking and eliminating expenses, reducing debt, and communicating with our partners and family help us work toward financial freedom.

Spend some time evaluating your retirement plans. There is a television commercial for a brokerage services firm where a man exclaims that he just closes his eyes and throws darts at his financial goals and hopes it sticks. This is sadly true for so many Americans. We need to evaluate and understand our investment options and make sure we are allocating the resources to the proper instruments so that when we are older, we can use these resources to accomplish our goals, dreams, and desires. We cannot assume that our retirement will just work itself out! We must commit ourselves to accomplishing our goals!

Physical Stewardship

Likewise, just as we take care of our financial resources, we should certainly take care of our bodies. Scripture tells us that our bodies are the temple of the Lord, so we should respect and take care of these temples. The benefits of physical fitness are endless and can enrich the quality of our lives tremendously. Let's explore how physical fitness can improve our pursuit of success, fulfillment, and purpose.

First, if we are physically fit, we just feel so much better. Our bodies and minds operate at a higher level. Our energy levels are improved, therefore our minds are sharper. Being physically active and fit improves our attitude, our confidence, and our creativity. We can work harder and longer. Additionally, by being physically fit, we can save a tremendous amount of money on life and medical insurance premiums. Also, we can prevent long-term health issues, as well as emotional and mental health issues. We only have this one body. It is our responsibility to take care of it and make it last as long as possible.

I was a smoker for over twenty years. I started smoking when I was maybe fifteen. The sad thing is I loved smoking. Those Marlboro lights were my constant companion. For twenty-two years, they were the first thing I looked for in the morning and the last thing I saw before I went to bed. As our daughter got older, she began to express mounting concerns about the effects of smoking. I brushed off her nagging for a long time. However, by the time I was thirty-five, it was really beginning to bother me. I could feel the effects of the years of smoking. I would become winded after minimal activity, I often had a nagging and persistent cough, and I often would end up with headaches late in the evening. However, none of these concerns alone were enough to make me quite.

When my dad was diagnosed with cancer in 1999, most likely attributable to smoking, I made the decision to quit. I did not want to see my wife and daughter go through the pain that I experienced with my dad's sickness. I made a promise to myself and to my family that I would quit as soon as the situation ended with my dad.

My father passed away in November of 1999, and we moved to the Nashville area in February of 2000. The timing was perfect for me to quit. I had a new job, a new life, and I was ready to kick the habit. So on March 15, 2000, I quit smoking. It was every bit as hard as I had always heard it was. I had a few setbacks and fell "off the wagon" a few times. But I refused to give up. When I failed and started back, I would visualize the positive effects of quitting and resolve to keep trying. I was finally able to quit. It has been many years since I quit smoking, and I now run, exercise, and feel better than I probably ever have in my life.

We all have weaknesses we battle regarding our health. Yours may be smoking, drinking, eating too much, or eating the wrong things. Whatever it may be, no matter what your age, I implore you to take action to get into shape and take control of your physical health. It is never too late to start. However, be patient and do not become frustrated.

When God presents us with opportunities for success, we need to be operating at optimum peak performance so we can be more efficient, effective, and successful. I gather from scripture that Joseph was very health conscious. I can envision him doing push-ups and sit-ups while he was in prison to pass the time. He was expecting greater things and wanted to be prepared to act. Now that I am older, I realize that time is a valuable asset, much like money, gold, and other treasures that should not be wasted. I possess a sense of urgency about everything.

Tithing/Giving

Certainly tithing and giving to others is commanded by God. There are countless verses in the Bible that support this. I will admit, I have struggled with tithing at times in my life. I could always find so many other things to do with that money we designated for tithing. Seems as if I always told myself, or rationalized for myself, that one day I would give back to God. But my wife has always been faithful in this discipline, and over the years she convinced me to give to God first. Never put God last when it comes to giving back to him. Additionally, we must insure our motivation behind tithing is appropriate. We do not tithe to God in expectations of some great blessing, or that it will be returned to us tenfold if we are faithful. I certainly do think God rewards those who are faithful to him, but we must give back to God out of respect and thanks for what he has already blessed us with.

Before we can be generous, we must first be frugal. We must first learn to save some of what we make, spend less than we make, and then give accordingly. If we have our financial house in order, we will have so much more to give back to God.

Oddly enough, the habits of people evidently have not changed very much over thousands of years. Apparently, the ancient Egyptians did not understand the concept of saving, as Joseph had to implement a savings plan for the grain.

Giving to or helping someone in need is a tremendous blessing that we should not rob ourselves of. Over the last few years, when we could, we have chosen various charities to give to. We saw a story on Dateline a few years ago about a food pantry in Ohio that was overwhelmed with needs during the height of the recession. We donated some money to them. Over the years, we have donated to children's hospitals, pregnancy centers, pet rescues, and special needs schools, along with many others. There is never a shortage of needs. You can give locally, regionally, or globally. I can truly say, for all that we have given, we have never seemed to miss the money.

Potiphar entrusted his household to Joseph because I believe that he recognized Joseph's commitment to stewardship. He saw how Joseph respected his property. He saw that Joseph took care of what he was in charge of and made a conscious effort to earn an appropriate return for Potiphar on his assets.

We should be good stewards of our employer's resources as well. The main reason we are hired as employees is because we will help them achieve their financial goals. We should work diligently, as Joseph did, to help our employers achieve those goals. Usually, we will be rewarded in proportion to what we contribute. Joseph understood this concept surrounding stewardship.

When Pharaoh appointed Joseph to second in command, Joseph immediately accepted his stewardship responsibilities, and he diligently pursued amassing the grain. Joseph understood that through building assets (in this case grain/feed), he would be able to minister to and help many in need. We need to think like Joseph regarding stewardship. I am not just referring to tithing or giving money to churches and charities. We are stewards over many various and diverse resources. Thinking strategically and critically will ensure that we utilize our resources to their fullest, hence, serving God's purpose to the fullest.

Additionally, stewardship encompasses so much more than just money. According to scripture, God gave man "dominion" over the animal kingdom and the earth. With that dominion, we have the responsibility of protecting these precious "God given" resources. My wife, daughter, and I are passionate about rescue animals. We have given three abandoned dogs forever homes to date.

We need to be mindful of our environment and treat our earth and our animals with reverence because we are stewards over them. Be mindful of the things we waste. Americans dump billions of tons of refuse in our landfills each year. We are so wasteful because we have always had an enormous supply of resources. However, the scars upon the climate and the earth reflect our lack of stewardship over the last couple of hundred years. I truly believe God wants us to protect all of our resources so the generations that follow us can enjoy them.

We should also be good stewards of our time. We all need down time to decompress, relax, and rest. However, when I truly evaluate how my time is spent, I can see so many opportunities to use my time more wisely.

I love college football. When autumn arrives, I usually spend four to five hours each Saturday watching the games. A few years ago, I began to think about all of the time I have wasted in my life watching football. In the grand scheme of eternity, does it really matter if one team beats another this year or if that team wins next year? There is nothing wrong with watching sports or spending time doing things we enjoy. However, there needs to be balance. Managing our time is a crucial aspect of stewardship. To experience complete success, we should be good stewards in all that we do. Work at maintaining an attitude of stewardship in everything.

Attribute VIII

Perseverance

Genesis 39:20-21 *Joseph's master took him and put him in prison, the place where the king's prisoners were confined. But while Joseph was there in prison, the Lord was with him; he showed him kindness and granted him favor in the eyes of the prison warden.*

After being sold into slavery by his very own brothers, Joseph was transported to a foreign land. The vision of his future was obscured by confounding disruptions and unplanned detours. Despite these setbacks, he eventually ended up serving in Potiphar's household. Joseph accepted this setback in life and concluded his only option was to press on.

After rising through the ranks and becoming head of Potiphar's household, he was falsely accused of attempted rape and sent to prison. Once again, Joseph's life took an unexpected turn. However, once again, he accepted his circumstances and earned additional responsibilities in jail. Joseph possessed perseverance.

As President Calvin Coolidge once said, "Nothing in this world can take the place of persistence. Talent will not; nothing is more common than unsuccessful people with talent. Genius will not; unrewarded genius is almost a proverb. Education will not; the world is full of educated derelicts. Persistence and determination alone are omnipotent."

As the president stated, there are two aspects to perseverance. One is persistence, the ability to stay focused on an ultimate goal regardless of life's diversions and distractions. This is the persistence aspect of perseverance. The second aspect is determination, withstanding and surviving, in a positive way, adversity and trials in life.

Over the years, volumes have been written about perseverance. Remaining resilient in the face of adversity is a noble pursuit. It does not matter who you are, where you live, or what your socio-economic background is. One thing everyone can count on is adversity. It does not discriminate or show favoritism. Everyone experiences disappointments and setbacks, some minor, some major.

One of the key differentiators between successful people and unsuccessful people is their response and reactions to adversity and diversions. Adversity, trials, and failures are crossroads in our lives. They are defining moments that demand defining responses. Do we throw in the towel on our hopes, dreams, goals, and aspirations when we have a setback, or do we plant our feet and continue toward the accomplishment of these dreams through our response to them?

What separates extraordinary people from ordinary people is how they respond to adversity. Are we debilitated when we experience adversity or trials? Having worked in sales for twenty plus years, I have certainly experienced the euphoria that comes along with "closing a deal," and I have experienced the bone-crushing defeat of losing a deal. I mentioned earlier that I used to mentor some of the new reps when they joined our company. One of the things I talked to them about most was how to deal with the rejections and disappointments that come with the business. I worked with one young lady who would become physically ill for a couple of days if she lost out on a proposal. The most successful sales people I have observed are those who brush off rejection and move forward with a "damn the torpedoes" mentality.

Adversity comes in many forms and severities. Losing a potential contract or client is minimal compared to the stress of losing a job, losing a loved one, being betrayed by someone we love and trust, or being the random victim of a senseless act or action. I have been through a variety of adversities and want to think I react and respond differently now than I did when I was younger.

Joseph dealt with many life-defining adversities. Being sold into slavery and being separated from his family ranks right up at the top of the stress meter. Being accused of a crime he did not commit and being sent to prison for that crime was another huge setback for Joseph. Although Genesis does not delve into specifics regarding how Joseph reacted to these events, I think we can conclude, and this is somewhat presumptive, that he was surely devastated emotionally by these events. It is only natural to experience periods of frustration, disappointment, and even temporary bouts of mild depression.

However, it is also apparent that Joseph regrouped, recommitted, and refused to let these derailments stop him from obtaining success, fulfillment, and purpose. Once again, the attributes work together and interact with each other. Possessing spiritual maturity (understanding God's nature), maintaining integrity, being content, having a support group of family and friends, etc., make handling adversity a little bit easier.

I will be the first to admit, even though I have worked in sales for twenty years, sometimes I get so discouraged and frustrated when deals fall through or do not close. I talk to some of the best salespeople I have ever known on a regular basis, and we all go through cycles where we just cannot seem to close a sale. This can be the case with any business or line of work.

Successful people are resilient and refuse to let themselves get down when things are moving slowly. Over the years, I have observed that great salespeople keep a healthy prospect "pipeline" because they have learned that sales are a numbers game. They understand that they will not close every deal. Therefore, they have contingencies in place so when something falls through, as it always will, they can move on to the next opportunity.

I believe the ability to handle adversity and trials improve in proportion to the level of our spiritual maturity. Having faith in God and understanding God's sovereignty in our lives at least makes trials and hardships more bearable. I am not suggesting that only Christians can handle hardships, but I do think it makes life's hardships easier to bear. I could not imagine going through my hardships without trusting in an omnipotent, all-knowing, all-caring God.

Attribute IX

Confidence

Genesis 41:15 *Pharaoh said to Joseph, "I had a dream, and no one can interpret it. But I have heard it said of you that when you hear a dream you can interpret it."*

Genesis 41:16 *"I cannot do it," Joseph replied to Pharaoh, "but God will give Pharaoh the answer he desires."*

Joseph understood the power Pharaoh possessed. With the wave of his hand, Joseph could have been put to death if Pharaoh did not like the interpretation Joseph provided. However, Joseph was sure and confident when he stood before Pharaoh. How? Because Joseph knew that God would provide the answers. Joseph's confidence came from God. When you trust that God is in control, your confidence will be unshakable.

One might think possessing confidence is contradictory to humbleness. I am not referring to an arrogant or boastful sense of confidence. Believers should possess a quite, unshakable confidence because we do have the Lord of the universe on our side. Real confidence will give us the edge we need to take action, be bolder, take chances, and so many other things we need to do to be successful. When we are confident, we are not indecisive. Joseph was confident because he knew God would ultimately be there for him. If we truly can keep this in mind, nothing can shake our confidence.

Confidence also comes from being knowledgeable. In sales, I have to possess an in-depth knowledge of the product or service I represent for me to sell it effectively. I want to know the strengths and weaknesses of my product or service, the strengths and weaknesses of my competitor's products and services, and I want to know how my products or services will help my client be more successful at what they do. The more I know about the topic I am discussing, the more confident I am. I have worked with many salespeople and observed many salespeople who did not put forth the effort to learn the intricate nuances of their products or services, much less that of their competitors. Usually, their performance suffered because they were not willing to learn the minutia of their products and services. You will possess a huge advantage over your competition, regardless of what you do, when you know what you are talking about.

Point being, we will all be more confident if we are constantly learning. I listened to a speaker once who talked of our education system here in the United States. He said that American kids went to school for twelve years back in the 1700s, just like they are required to go for twelve years today. However, the lifespan of Americans in that era was only 35-40 years of age. Students went to school for approximately half of their lives in many cases. Today, we still only require twelve years of education, but our people are living well into their seventies, eighties, and nineties. God did not intend for us to go to school for twelve to sixteen years and then quit learning for the rest of our lives. Our world is changing at warp speed. If we are constantly learning new skills, perspectives, and abilities, we will be much more confident, competitive, and successful. I have heard a lot of sales trainers suggest that good sales people should be "generalists," where you know a little about a lot rather than knowing a lot about what you are selling. I understand and agree with the concept that we need to expand our knowledge about many topics, but I think the person who is a "subject matter expert" will always excel at whatever their endeavor is. The more you know, the more confident you will be.

Regardless of your vocation or your circle of influence, you will be more confident if you are knowledgeable about your subject. I suspect Joseph spent much time learning and gaining an understanding of the things he would later be in charge of. Competence creates confidence. Joseph, no more than a farmer, is called upon to interpret the king of Egypt's dreams. Genesis does not suggest that Joseph stumbled, fumbled, and mumbled his way through this conversation with Pharaoh. If Pharaoh had sensed uncertainty or a lack of confidence in Joseph's voice, he may not have believed in his interpretation and could have sent him back to prison thinking he was a lunatic or a fraud. Joseph was confident when his opportunity presented itself. We only get one opportunity for a first impression.

We all go through times when our confidence gets beat down. A series or chain of defeats can drain us of our morale, self-esteem, and confidence. These periods of defeat are normal. We must be cautious not to develop a defeatist attitude. If you find you're adapting a defeatist mentality, step back, review, and relive some of your past accomplishments and victories. Remember the exhilaration that came from those victories or wins. Re-create the sights, sounds, and smells of those moments, and dwell on them. Then re-commit to confidence. Confidence, or the lack of, is reflected in our body language, our demeanor, and our eye contact. People sense whether we are confident or not. It is crucial that we maintain our confidence even when we experience defeat.

Ironically, even after many years in sales, I still sometimes struggle with confidence. If I lose out on a sale, I often question myself and wonder if I did something wrong. It is extremely challenging for me to emotionally disconnect myself from a loss. I continue to work through this challenge all the time. In the end, I think it is okay to replay a situation mentally to see if you could have done something differently, but then we have to move on and shake it off.

We all seem to go through periods of consistent victories, where we seem to be on top of the world and everything is hitting on all cylinders. Then, there are periods of time where things seem to go against us, as if we cannot do anything right. We need to understand that these times will pass. We cannot let it rattle our confidence. We have to brush it off and move on.

Additionally, confident people possess good interpersonal skills. They possess the ability to connect with others. As much as any trait, Joseph was extremely effective at connecting with others. This provided him the confidence he needed to be successful.

Finally, confidence comes from God. We must remember the God of the universe is on our side. Joseph had complete trust that God would provide the confidence he needed to succeed. He knew God had given him the insight to interpret dreams. Therefore, when called before Pharaoh, he had no doubt that God would provide the wisdom.

Positive Attitude

Maintaining a positive attitude is crucial to developing the confidence we need to be successful. Over the years, I have observed many successful men and women who, despite setbacks and obstacles, are able to maintain an unshakable positive attitude. We cannot let every little obstacle defeat us. We must maintain a victorious attitude, not an attitude of defeat or dejection.

Recently there has been a series of public service announcements aired on a local television channel. These commercials emphasize the importance of positive traits and are geared at young viewers. One in particular shows a young boy alone on a baseball field. He is tossing up the ball and swinging at it with a bat. He tosses the ball the first time and exclaims, "I am the greatest batter in the world!" He misses the ball and it hits the ground. He whispers, "Strike one." He picks up the ball and tosses it up again, exclaiming, "I am the greatest batter in the world!" He swings and misses again. He then mutters, "Strike two." He picks up the ball for the third time, tosses it up, and shouts, "I am the greatest batter in the world!" He swings and misses for the third time. He looks defeated for a moment and shouts out, "I must be the greatest pitcher in the world!"

Sometimes we need that childlike confidence that can only come from God. If we fail at something, it must mean we are good at something else. Being confident is crucial to experiencing success. I am referring to a calm, humble confidence, not an arrogant, obnoxious confidence. We, like Joseph, must ultimately be confident in ourselves, but more confident that God is guiding our paths.

Attribute X

Courage

Genesis 41:28-30 *"It is just as I said to Pharaoh: God has shown Pharaoh what he is about to do. Seven years of great abundance are coming throughout the land of Egypt, but seven years of famine will follow them. Then all the abundance in Egypt will be forgotten, and the famine will ravage the land."*

Once again, Joseph has to tell the king of Egypt the good news and the bad news. Once again Joseph understood Pharaoh possessed the power to kill him if he did not like his answer. However, Joseph possessed courage. He told Pharaoh exactly what was going to happen. He did not attempt to sugar coat the future out of fear Pharaoh might react negatively to the news. Like confidence, courage is paramount to our success, fulfillment, and purpose.

Do not confuse courage with confidence. Confidence is an inner sense of being sure of yourself in a given situation and knowing you will respond in a positive way. Courage is stepping out of a comfort zone and into an unsure environment to achieve or obtain what it is you seek, and sometimes to tell it like it is.

I read a great quote recently in Success Magazine from the actor Rob Lowe. In an interview with a writer for the magazine, he said, "The comfort zone is the first instinct. A lot of people are like, 'I have some success. I feel like that should be enough.' Once you gravitate toward comfort, you tend to assume the status quo, and that can leave you unprepared for the moment when your world tanks." Later, he goes on to say, "To get out of your comfort zone means to stretch, to extend, to reach beyond what you've had success doing. And that can be difficult. Do not let yourself get caught in the "stagnation quo."

I am not saying we should take irrational, sporadic actions with no fear or thought for the future, but, we must be willing to extend our reach if we want to reach new heights.

A few years ago I watched a movie called *"Collateral."* Tom Cruise plays a sinister murderer who flies into Los Angeles one night to assassinate several targets. Jamie Foxx plays an unlucky cab driver who picks up Tom Cruise's character at LAX and ultimately is forced to drive him all over the city during the night.

As a subplot to the movie, Jamie's character (Max) has always dreamed of starting his own limo service. However, after twelve years, he is still driving the cab. Max had never taken the leap of faith and started the business. He rationalized his inaction by throwing up seemingly insurmountable obstacles. Like so many of us, his dream remained just that, a distant dream.

In an early scene from the movie, Tom Cruise's character (Vincent) quizzes Jamie's character (Max) about how long he has been driving the cab. Jamie's character (Max) tells Vincent that he has been driving the cab for twelve years, but the cabbie job is just temporary until he can start his own limo company. Vincent chuckles and observes that twelve years is a long time for a temporary job. Later in the night, during a heated exchange between the two, the following conversation occurs:

VINCENT (Tom Cruise)

With your paper towels...a bottle of 409...a limo company someday. How much you got saved?

MAX (Jamie Foxx)

None of your business!

VINCENT (Tom Cruise)

Your business plan, someday? Someday my dream will come true?

One night you'll wake up and discover it all flipped on
you. Suddenly you're old. And it didn't happen. And it
never will. Because you never were going to do it
anyway. The dream on the horizon became yesterday
and got lost. Then you'll kid yourself. It never could
have been anyway, and you'll recede it into memory,
and zone out in a Barcalounger with daytime TV on for
the rest of your life.

Don't talk to me about killing, you're doing it to
yourself. In this yellow and orange prison, bit by bit,
everyday.

All it ever took was a down payment on a Lincoln Town
Car. What are you still doing in this cab?

I know this is just a script from a movie, but there are some
great points in this brief conversation. One, are the "barriers of
entry" to achieving our dreams real or self-imposed by us? In
Max's mind, buying that Lincoln Town Car was an overwhelming
obstacle that he could not overcome. Vince pointed out that all
Max really had to do was make a down payment on a Town Car
and he could have realized his dream. Out of his fear to step
outside his comfort zone, Max had created insurmountable
obstacles to achieving his dream, when in reality, all he really had
to do was make a down payment on a car.
    Vince also makes another great observation. Max had never
mapped out a real concise business plan. Someday? For a dream
to become a reality, we must have goals, and goals must be
specific with specific timeframes. Goals are dreams with dead-
lines. No wonder he did not have the courage to take the leap
from cab driver to limo driver.
    If we are intentional in our planning, we will be prepared for
backups, the plan "B's", and the contingencies. The courage
needed to execute on a vision will be easier to draw upon if we
have tangible goals and milestones set in place, and a specific
time period identified to work toward. Simply wishing for a
dream to become a reality is futile.

Max's situation really encapsulates the challenge of developing courage. Yes, some people are born with courage. Some people, like Joseph, had no choice but to be courageous. Regardless of your dream, it will demand courage.

How many of us are still driving our yellow and orange cab because we were afraid to take a chance on our dream? We convince ourselves there are too many obstacles in the way. If only we had more money, we could do it. If only we had more time, we could pursue it, and on and on we go. In reality, just as Vincent told Max, all you have to do is make a down payment on a Town Car and you are in business.

If we truly want to succeed, we must overcome our fears and acquire courage. Once again, I am not saying we should do something rash or spur of the moment. We should plan, and plan carefully. But, sadly, like Max, too often our dream is no more than just an escape from our reality. We never really had the courage, the faith, the confidence to take that leap to begin with.

We truly are creatures of habit. Once we get comfortable with a situation, a job, a position, or a relationship, we become afraid to change it. We discuss this deeper in the attribute of adaptability. Joseph had no alternative but to face his fears. He was thrust into a strange land with strange people and strange customs. Joseph had no past experience, resume, training, or professional mentoring, or pedigree to step into the role of head of household for Potiphar. However, Joseph knew he had to seize the moment. Later, the skills he learned while running Potiphar's household served him well when he became second in command in the prison guard. Then, later, those skills prepared him for second in command to Pharaoh. When Pharaoh handed him the reigns, he took them. He showed no obvious signs of apprehension or fear of failure. He was courageous. Joseph possessed a sense of urgency and laser-like focus on what needed to be done to be successful, and he beat down any thoughts of failure; not mistakes, but failures. Joseph certainly possessed courage, and we can develop courage.

One of the most humiliating experiences of my life happened back in 1991. I was taking a banking class at night with several of my colleagues. On the last night of the class, we had to get up and give a five to seven minute presentation to the entire class on any topic in banking. I had chosen to do my presentation on the Federal Deposit Insurance Corporation, or the FDIC.

I had not given a pubic presentation since high school some ten years earlier. When I got up in front of the class, I experienced a case of stage fright like never before. My voice trembled, my hands were shaking, and I painfully floundered through the presentation for what seemed like an eternity. After finishing, I scurried back to my seat for the rest of the night. If possible, I would have climbed into a hole and never came out.

I did not want to go back to work the next morning because I would have to come face to face with those same colleagues who had nailed their presentations the night before. However, I had no choice but to go back to work and face the humiliation. My co-workers and classmates were all very gracious and kind and never mentioned the incident again.

From that point forward, anytime I even thought that I would have to speak to a crowd larger than two, I would run from the situation. I was determined to never go through that humiliation again. Just the thoughts of having to stand in front of a group of people literally caused me to be nauseous. For almost five years, I managed to avoid having to speak in front of large groups. Oftentimes I would read job descriptions for higher paying opportunities within and outside the company; however, if I saw any mention of speaking in large groups as part of the description, I would walk away from the opportunity. I received a promotion in 1996 and knew that inevitably I would be confronted with doing a presentation again because training/presentations/seminars were an important aspect of the job. Sure enough, I was asked to give a presentation to approximately thirty high ranking executives, branch managers, and other officers for a customer bank of mine. Needless to say, I was petrified.

However, I decided to dissect that event and determine what went wrong. Did I experience stage fright simply because I had not given a presentation since high school? I replayed the events of that night over and over in my mind. What I realized in the end was, I had not prepared for the presentation, and so, it was only reasonable to assume I would have been anxious.

I made a decision to face this fear head on and to overcome it. I went out and bought a book on public speaking. I read how I needed to rehearse the presentation over and over, and how I needed to know the presentation inside and out so I would be confident and courageous when my next speaking opportunity came about.

I quickly put my presentation together for the bank meeting, rehearsed dozens of times, and video-taped the rehearsals to see it from the audiences view. When I went to bed the night before the meeting, I felt a peace and confidence that I was prepared this time.

The meeting was on a Friday morning, and I rehearsed the presentation one more time in my hotel room that morning before arriving at the bank. When I was called upon for the presentation, it went very well. Since that time, I have given countless presentations, conducted seminars, and facilitated meetings to groups ranging in size from ten to fifty. I admit, I still get anxious about speaking, but in a good way. If I am truly prepared for the presentation, it usually goes very well. That failure was painful, but I learned some very valuable lessons from it.

That incident was a defining moment for me. I decided to overcome the anxiety and fear that was hindering me. It would have been easy to run and hide from the fear forever. Ultimately, I had to face it. Usually, if we truly dissect the fear and confront it, we can overcome it.

In 1999, my wife decided to go into business for herself. She had worked several years for a CPA in our hometown, and she was burned out and wanted to go in a different direction. It was a scary proposition. We were accustomed to having her salary, in addition to mine, to meet our budget. After much prayer, discussion, and more prayer, she decided to take the plunge.

She quickly learned that she was really good at her job of keeping books and accounting. However, what she feared most was going out and cold calling on businesses to send her work. In the beginning, she would stress herself out almost to the point of making herself sick when she had to go out and call on businesses. Yet, she understood that if she was going to make it on her own, she had no choice. She encountered the usual frustrations, rejection, and discouragement that go along with cold calling.

For some time, I thought she might give it up and go back to the comforts of a full-time job. However, she relented, and kept calling, and she kept overcoming the fears she had of calling on these businesses. Sure enough, after a few months, she started getting more and more work. She developed the courage to overcome her fear because she wanted this opportunity and the positive trade-offs that came with it. She was willing to work through the fear to experience success at this endeavor.

We must overcome fears in our lives to reach our full potential. Joseph did not have the luxury of running from fear. He was thrust headfirst into uncertainty when he was sold into slavery. Ultimately, he knew he had to overcome fear and develop courage to achieve true success.

As I mentioned earlier, I got to travel to China back in 2005 with a group of Christian business leaders to meet with and mentor some Chinese Christian business owners. It was a tremendous experience. We got to visit the great historical sites like the Great Wall and Tiananmen Square. We also learned about the culture and rich history of China.

We also learned that it is not illegal to be a Christian in China as long as you belong to one of the "state approved" Christian churches. The Christian doctrines of these "state approved" churches are diluted with communist philosophies. Thus, most Chinese Christians choose to worship in secret or "underground" churches at great risk and peril. We learned that the government can, and often does, persecute citizens for participating in these churches. We heard horror stories of people who had been beaten, imprisoned, and sent away to remote prison camps for years for disobeying the law.

One night, we even attended a secret church service. It was a very scary and emotional event. Watching these people who were so excited about Christ risk their lives was a humbling experience. Maybe you love something more when it comes at a cost. Nonetheless, these brave citizens have developed courage like most Americans, including myself, will never have to know. I think this is the kind of courage Joseph possessed, and we can possess it if we develop it.

We need to develop courage for many reasons. When we see someone being wronged, or something unethical that we should expose, we should have the courage to stand forward and denounce it. There will be situations in our lives where we have to have courage. Evaluate the fears in your life and determine if they are legitimate or exaggerated. Determine if fear is obstructing or preventing you from achieving a dream, experiencing success, or achieving fulfillment and purpose.

So you have had fears or lacked courage? Join the gang. Read the Bible. Countless heroes from scripture experienced fear: Abraham, Moses, David, Samson, Esther, Jonah, Peter, Jesus. Yes, even Jesus in the Garden of Gethsemane feared what was before him, but all of these people trusted God to get them through their fear and developed the courage to be successful.

Anxiety/Stress

One only has to watch the news for a few moments to see plenty of reasons to be anxious about the world we live in. Mass shootings, climate change, political upheaval around the globe, the European economic crisis, the fiscal cliff, and the list could go on and on and on. Sometimes it seems as if the world is in total chaos. The only certain thing in life is uncertainty.

I am sure Joseph faced anxiety, as everyone who has ever lived faces anxiety. It is crucial, for us to be successful, to manage our anxieties. Joseph trusted that God was in ultimate control of his life and this world, and trusted that God would provide and protect him. This is all we can do. If anxiety becomes unmanageable, it can often result in alcohol abuse, drug abuse, or other "crutches," and it will eventually take a tremendous toll on our physical and emotional health. There is an abundance of resources available on how to manage anxiety. If you struggle with anxiety, seek help and overcome it.

One of my favorite pastors is Steve Brown of Key Life Ministries. Steve has had a daily radio broadcast on Moody Radio for years called Key Life. He possesses a deep, thunderous voice ideal for radio. He is also a professor at a college in Florida where his ministry is based. Steve grew up in Western North Caroline not too far from where I grew up. I have heard him tell this story several times about the Cherokee Indians who have a reservation in the foothills of the Smoky Mountains. In the past, when

Cherokee boys reached the age of manhood or puberty, they were taken out into the woods by their fathers. They would then be left to spend a night alone in the vast forest. One can only imagine the fear that a young boy would experience in the dark of the night. The rustling of the leaves or the crack of a branch in the distance only added fear and panic to the experience. At last, when the sun finally rose over the peaks of the mountains, the first thing the boy saw was his father in a nearby tree. He had spent the entire night watching over his son making sure he was safe, yet unknown to the young boy. Steve reminds us that God is kind of like that. There will be times when we are scared; times when it seems that we are alone facing the dark forest of life by ourselves. But one day, we will know that God was there the whole time, watching over us and protecting us. Fear is a common thing in life. Respect it and learn from it, but do not be paralyzed by it. God tells us time and time again that we can overcome the fear in our lives if we trust him.

Attribute XI

Communication

Genesis 41:41 *So Pharaoh said to Joseph, "I hereby put you in charge of the whole land of Egypt."*

After consulting with his immediate staff, Pharaoh decided to put Joseph in charge of the famine project and named him second in command. I do not believe Pharaoh simply did this because Joseph was the one who could interpret his dreams. I think Pharaoh recognized that Joseph possessed, among the other attributes, the crucial ability to communicate.

Good communication skills are crucial to experiencing complete success. Good communication skills are crucial to developing relationships. As a matter of fact, good communication skills are probably the most important life skill we can learn to differentiate ourselves from others, yet it remains one of the worst skills of so many people today. In our hectic pace, we hardly slow down long enough, engage with someone long enough, and listen long enough to truly communicate.

While the digital age has been incredible in terms of quicker productivity and connectivity, it has done little to improve true communication. In fact, it has worsened and enabled an already poor ability to communicate. I know I talk about adaptability in this book, and yes, email and texting is appropriate and efficient at times for a quick response, quick answer, or confirmation. But ultimately, to be effective, we need to have real verbal conversations with other people.

I have worked with people, had customers, and have friends who literally cannot sit down in a restaurant for thirty minutes and eat lunch without constantly looking at their Blackberries or I-phones to see if they have a text or a message. Usually, the messages are frivolous or insignificant. This distraction has truly become an obsession.

A few years ago, I recommended a friend I knew for a job with the company I worked for. His resume was impeccable. His background and experience were perfect for the role. He interviewed several times with human resources and the hiring manager, and they were ready to make him an offer. The night before they were going to offer him the position, they asked him to go to dinner. The job offer was simply a formality. They arrived at the restaurant, and the guy spent the whole evening reading and sending emails, firing off text messages, and appeared completely disengaged and completely oblivious to them and the conversations they were trying to have with him. The hiring manager was insulted, and the next morning the manager and human resource manager decided to go in a different direction, and they hired someone else for the position.

When the hiring manager told me about his behavior, I was shocked and disappointed. This friend called me a few days later and asked me if I knew what the status of the job offer was. He was perplexed as to why our human resources manager had not called him and made the job offer to him. I could not bring myself to telling him he had lost out on the opportunity simply because he appeared indifferent during the interaction with the managers.

No matter how advanced our society becomes techno-logically, nothing will ever take the place of good old face-to-face, verbal communication. My current manager constantly reminds our sales team to never default to email or texting when a phone call or face-to-face meeting is appropriate or possible. I have to admit, I am the worst offender. I feel much more comfortable firing off an email to a prospect about the status of a proposal than I do picking up the phone and calling them. It is much easier to email a prospect about a meeting than to pick up the phone and anguish through an awkward phone call. However, real communication, either over the phone or in person, is the most effective way to convey a message.

Joseph recognized and understood the importance of real communication. In Genesis 42:23, when Joseph's brothers approached him the first time to buy food, he spoke to them through an interpreter. In the time that Joseph had spent in Egypt, he had learned to speak the Egyptian language. Joseph knew if he was to assume responsibility in Egypt, he would have to be able to communicate with the Egyptians. So he learned their language and spoke their lingo.

To be successful in any endeavor, we must possess the ability to communicate with those we are hoping to reach for whatever purpose it may be. If you want to be a great preacher, you must be able to communicate. If you want to be the CEO of a Fortune 500 company, you must be able to communicate. If you want to be an effective parent, you must be able to communicate.

The good news is good communication skills can be learned. We are not born with great communication skills. Learning to communicate effectively does take effort and requires us to change our paradigms about communication. For whatever reason, so many people think good communication comes from doing all the talking, but the best communicators are good listeners. The most important aspect of communication is listening to the person we are trying to communicate with. I am amazed at how challenging this is for so many people, and I am often guilty of it myself. I have seen countless sales people sabotage their own efforts by talking too much during a presentation or discussion with a prospect. It is easy to do because the adrenalin is flowing, and you want to appear knowledgeable to the client. However, the best way to sell, or communicate, is simply to listen first before you talk.

Think of a volatile situation you have been in. Assume someone is upset about something you did or your company did or did not do. I have had these conversations with customers in banking for years. Usually, if we listen to the person who is upset and let them make their case, we begin to defuse the situation immediately. However, if we cut them off, interrupt them, and interject our opinion before they are finished, they generally become more and more agitated.

My father was friends with a man back in Cleveland, Tennessee during the 1980s. This man ran a small detail shop where he cleaned up cars for local dealers. He was an extremely hard worker who managed to make a meager living with this shop. Somehow, he became friends with an executive for one of the largest auto auction chains in the country. This executive asked David if he would have any interest in moving to Atlanta, Georgia to supervise the detailing operations at this auction. The opportunity was incredible. Not only would he receive a generous regular salary, the job would also provide insurance, retirement benefits, and all of those perks that small business owners often cannot afford. After discussing with his family, he accepted the opportunity.

He moved to Atlanta eager and excited about the opportunity. However, he quickly learned that the role would be more challenging than he ever anticipated. David was a middle-aged, white male. Every one of the men who worked in the detail shop was young African-American men. Most of them were from the urban neighborhoods surrounding Atlanta. Needless to say, David had a very difficult time communicating with these men. They used slang and lingo that was foreign to David, and he used slang and lingo that was foreign to them. Among many dynamics that were difficult in the situation, communication between David and the men was horrible. David quickly realized that he would not be able to garner the respect and authority from these young men he needed to have to manage the group effectively.

David called a friend from Cleveland, Tennessee, a young African-American man that had worked at his detail shop, and asked him if he would be interested in coming to work at the auction serving as a supervisor over the detailing operation. The gentleman accepted, moved to Atlanta, and worked under David, supervising the men in the detail shop. Immediately, the dynamics changed drastically. Because this man was able to communicate, resonate, and relate with these men, he and David enjoyed much success in the role. David realized he needed someone under him who could communicate with these guys, and by selecting the perfect candidate, the operation was a huge success. David recognized the crucial importance of communication and understood he could not be an effective leader without it.

Attribute XII

Ambition

Genesis 39:6 *So he (Potiphar) left in Joseph's care everything he had; with Joseph in charge, he did not concern himself with anything.*

It is apparent that Potiphar recognized many good qualities in Joseph. Potiphar recognized his honesty, his trustworthiness, his vision, the fact that God was with Joseph, his discipline, and his courage, to name a few. Potiphar also recognized that Joseph possessed ambition. Because Potiphar recognized the ambition in Joseph, he knew his wealth would multiply. In every situation he was in, Joseph excelled because he possessed the crucial attribute of ambition.

Do not confuse ambition with motivation. A person can have lofty motivations and only seek to do what is truly good and right, yet not possess the ambition to see their goals fulfilled. However, ambition is the drive to achieve and accomplish certain goals and to see the motivations put into action. You must possess some desire to be successful and understand the sacrifices that must be given to achieve certain goals.

You can poll anyone who has experienced success in the workplace, arts, athletics, or any other aspect of life, and every one of them, without fail, will consistently point out that they worked hard to achieve success. There is no shortcut around it. There is no path to dodge it. Anything worth doing will require hard work and ambition. No hurdle, no obstacle, or no limitation can stop someone who is willing to work hard enough. They can achieve anything. The attribute of ambition has lifted many from the chokehold of poverty, from the grip of limitations, and the constraints of social, racial, and ethnic attitudes. Possess ambition, and you have catapulted yourself into an elite class of unique people.

Sadly, so many people want the results that success brings, but so few are really willing to roll up their sleeves and put in the hard work that is required to succeed. Joseph went to work in Potiphar's household as no more than a foreign slave. But he excelled to a desired position because he was willing to work harder and longer than the other servants.

When I decided to go back to College in 2009 and finish my bachelor's degree, I knew I wanted the degree. I also recognized the sacrifices required to obtain it. The pursuit of that goal would cost me four hours a night, one night a week, for eighteen to twenty months. It would also cost me a sizable amount of money. It would also cost me countless hours on weekends and nights in hotel rooms working on essays and research papers, but I was determined to finally achieve that goal.

However, no matter how tired I was, no matter how overwhelming balancing work, home life, and school at the same time was, despite the distractions I encountered while pursuing the degree, including one bank failure and two job changes, I never lost sight of the end goal, which was to finish that degree. As much as I sought it, I had to muster the ambition and drive to finish it. It was not always easy, but I never considered quitting, for once in my life.

Joseph obviously possessed ambition. While Joseph was content in his present circumstances, he was not content to only serve as a slave in Potiphar's house. While he was content in his present circumstances while he was in prison, he was not content to be an average inmate and rose to a role of leadership in that environment. While he was content to be second in command in Egypt, he not only stored grain for the drought, he worked to ensure the government profited during a time of extreme duress.

To be successful at whatever it is we choose, we must want to achieve it. It takes ambition. How many times have we watched or listened to our favorite singer or musician and thought we wish that could have been us? But do we really wish for that? Would we have the ambition to practice guitar, piano, or whatever it is for six to seven hours a day while other kids were playing in the yard and having fun? Would we have the ambition to load everything we own up in a car and drive to Nashville or Los Angeles for a chance to play in a bar band for possibly the rest of our lives, never knowing if we would really achieve success?

Or maybe we see our favorite actor or actress and dream of living the exotic and privileged life they live. But would we be ambitious enough to move to Hollywood, work odd jobs in restaurants, and work for free in theatres and plays for years to hone the craft of acting, just for a remote shot at an acting job, when one in a million succeed? Not everyone possessed the ambition and drive to achieve these goals.

Perhaps your goals for success are not quite so lofty, but nonetheless, we must possess ambition to achieve anything in life. Simply wishing for an opportunity to happen is wishful thinking. Very seldom does the thing we hope to achieve simply fall out of the sky and into our lives. I am reminded of the joke where the man said, "People say I have no ambition. That's not true. When I win the lottery, I am going to do a lot of things." As ridiculous as this sounds, sometimes it is not far from what we think. We think the stars must line up just right before we pursue something, or at least that is the excuse we use. If we wait for the perfect time, or if certain things have to occur before we pursue our dream, they will likely never come true.

Joseph had the foresight to see he would one day be a great leader, but he did not sit around waiting for it happen or assuming he would wake up one day and it would simply fall in his lap. Instead of letting success come to him, he chased and caught it.

Recently on ESPN, I saw some video of new Ohio State Buckeyes' head coach Urban Meyer talking to his players during practice. Urban made a great statement to his new team. He said, "It is so easy to be average." What an observation. Nothing is easier than being average at a job. You show up on time, do nothing more than what is expected, get paid, and go home. Then, we wonder why we get passed up for promotion. We are insulted at our average pay raises for our average performances, or maybe we are perplexed when we get let go from our jobs during the first round of lay-offs.

We live and work in a competitive global economy. If we do nothing more than average work, we will never achieve anything more than average results. Ambitious people, like Joseph, look beyond the immediate task to see if it can be done better, more efficiently, and more effectively. Ambitious people look for ways to work smarter, not necessarily harder.

In 1989, I accepted an entry level position at a bank sorting checks on third shift. One of the guys who trained me had done this same job for ten years. As I talked with him that first night, I wondered why he had kept working third shift so long. Why, if he had the opportunity, had he not moved into another position over this much time? That night, as he explained sorting the checks, I asked him why we sorted certain checks a certain way, and he said, "I don't know, and I don't ask. I just sort the checks." Then, I realized why he was still in this position. He did not possess the curiosity or the interest in why things were being done the way they were being done. He just showed up and did them the same way. There is nothing wrong with that mentality; I just think it limits your potential. I have always wanted to know why things are done the way they are done, and what would be the impact, for better or for worse, if they are done differently. I suspect Joseph observed and evaluated certain processes and questioned and tested new ways of achieving results. He was ambitious, he was curious, and he obtained success.

Increase Your Value

I mentioned earlier in the book that you will always earn in proportion to the value you bring to your organization. It does not matter if you work for yourself or for a large corporation. Therefore, it is crucial that you identify ways to increase your value. I implore you to learn new skills, whether it be computer skills, a new language, or an advanced degree; something that will differentiate you from everyone else. Competition is strong and will continue to only get stronger. You can only stand out from the competition if you know more and bring more value to your position. Additionally, resources have never been more abundant and cheaper to access than they are now. You can take free courses online, complete degree programs online; listen to audio CDs, and download apps that teach you skills.

I must confess, I am a "NPR" junkie. I listen to National Public Radio everywhere I go. Everyday there are so many interesting stories regarding political, economic, cultural, and world events. It is like a perpetual radio university. I do not always necessarily agree with their slant or their opinions, but I would say I have learned more about the world we live in by listening to NPR than any other source of information I am aware of. We spend a lot of idle time commuting or traveling. We should put this time to productive use.

As I mentioned earlier, I believe Joseph was constantly honing his skills and abilities in anticipation of what God had in store for him. He yearned for success and prepared for it. Make yourself more valuable than you are now. Doing this will not only help you succeed in the professional world, but it will equip and enable you to be more successful in all walks of life.

Attribute XIII

Discipline

Genesis 41:46-49 *Joseph was thirty years old when he entered the service of Pharaoh king of Egypt. And Joseph went out from Pharaoh's presence and traveled throughout Egypt. During the seven years of abundance the land produced plentifully. Joseph collected all the food produced in those seven years of abundance in Egypt and stored it in the cities. In each city he put the food grown in the fields surrounding it.*

Not only did Joseph possess the strategic vision of storing up the grain during the prosperous years, he stuck to his plan and made sure there was no deviation from the plan. Joseph was disciplined. He recognized the importance of discipline.

How many times have you observed and admired someone who seemed to be so disciplined? They get up at four AM and run five miles. They train for years and climb Mount Everest. They always turn down dessert at dinner, whatever it may be. They never seem to indulge in anything that the rest of us cannot seem to walk away from.

Being disciplined in every aspect of our lives is crucial to being a success for so many reasons. Being a disciplined person generally results in accomplishing more in everything we do. However, I believe discipline is generally perceived as something you have to be born with. I believe discipline is an attribute you can acquire, improve, and build upon.

Successful people recognize that discipline is a skill you acquire, strengthen, and nurture. I am not saying you have to run a marathon to be successful. I am not saying you have to climb Mount Everest to be a success. But if you truly look at successful people, you will see that they always possess discipline. Discipline is not something you just flick a switch and have. It starts with small steps. Identify some weaknesses in your life. Then, begin taking strategic steps toward eliminating destructive habits and implementing positive habits, and you will see that discipline can become easier.

Think about how much more success you can experience with discipline. People who exercise regularly, eat healthier, and sleep the right amount of sleep are so much more effective. You feel better, so you think better, and you perform at optimum peak. Developing discipline results in a richer, more fulfilling experience and existence. It permeates, resonates, and reflects in everything we do. We become better and more successful at everything we do when we practice discipline in all areas of our lives.

Likewise, apply discipline on your job. When you are at work, work. Do not fall victim to time erasers that waste the time you spend at your job. I have a friend who works for a large bank in Kentucky. Due to some recent changes in his responsibilities, he spends almost an hour and a half commuting to and from work. However, he has told me that when he gets to the office, he attacks his tasks with a focused effort that he never possessed before. When he is at work, he works; when it is time to leave, he leaves. He wants to get home at a reasonable hour and does not want to waste one minute while he is at the office.

He told me he often skips lunch or eats a small lunch in a break room so he can accomplish his tasks and get out of the office at a reasonable time so he can be home by six thirty or seven o'clock in the evening. He told me that when he worked only twenty minutes from home, he would often waste countless hours chatting, eating, surfing the net, or whatever, but now, he wants to accomplish as much as he can while he is at work so he can get home.

In regards to physical discipline, think of the rewards of living a healthy lifestyle. By losing weight, quitting smoking, eating healthier, and exercising more, we will not only feel better, but we may reduce our health insurance costs. These savings can be used to achieve other goals, and the benefits go on and on. The key to developing discipline is to take small steps. Each success builds on success, and the attribute of discipline is obtained. Like any other skill, it requires constant work to retain and expand the art of discipline. You cannot obtain it, put it on a shelf for a couple of years, and simply call on it when desired. Discipline has to be engrained in your daily life.

If you need to lose thirty pounds to be at your desired or recommended weight, set small obtainable goals and recognize and accept that it will take time to achieve the goal. Too many times, we get too impatient and give up on discipline all together. Discipline can be obtained, but it takes work.

Attribute XIV

Balance

Genesis 43:24-25 *The steward took the men into Joseph's house, gave them water to wash their feet and provided fodder for their donkeys. They prepared their gifts for Joseph's arrival at noon, because they had heard that they were to eat there.*

Never forget that success takes hard work, and lots of it. However, it is absolutely crucial that we possess an understanding of balance. Without balance, we focus too much time and attention to one aspect of our lives and neglect another. It is a daunting juggling act, but the truly successful people are those who integrate balance into their lives.

I have seen countless marriages end and relationships with children or other loved ones strained because one spouse or the other was so focused on work that they neglect the ones who are most important to them. It is truly a tragedy when we focus all of efforts on our work to the point where our loved ones feel neglected. Likewise, we cannot focus all of our time on our marriage, hobbies, sports, etc., or our careers may suffer. It truly takes a focused effort to balance everything in life.

At least in Joseph's day, once he was home for the evening, he probably was not distracted by work until he returned the next day. Unfortunately for us, undivided attention to anything is a challenge within itself due to the deluge of distractions. When we do finally get home, we are constantly reading text messages, emails, checking Facebook, checking Twitter, checking our fantasy league scoreboard, checking the stock market ticker, or checking the CNN news alert. No wonder attention deficit disorder is at epidemic levels. When we get home, whenever that may be, we should shut down the phones, the internet, and the television, and spend quality time with our families. If not, we are present simply physically and not emotionally, and our relationships will suffer. Our minds and bodies were designed to have balance. That is why we burn out if we stay focused on something too long.

Some of my fondest memories as a child are the vacations and trips my family took. During that time, my father would shut his business completely down for two weeks, usually around the fourth of July. We would load up the station wagon and go to the beaches of Florida, Alabama, Mississippi, or Louisiana. We drove out west to the Grand Canyon and White Sands, New Mexico. We visited the Petrified Forest in Arizona and every small town in between. Once, we drove all the way to Acapulco, Mexico. We saw the mountain town of Tasco, home of the Mexican silver mines, we saw the cliff divers at Acapulco, and we attended an Aztec Indian festival in Mexico City.

Often on weekends, my parents would load up the car and just take off on an unplanned, completely spontaneous adventure. We spent a weekend at Callaway Gardens in Georgia. We visited the "little White House" in Warm Springs, Georgia where Franklin Roosevelt set up a camp for children with polio. We visited the house where he died while being painted by an artist. We visited the Grand Ole Opry in Nashville. We hiked a section of the Appalachian Trail in the Smokey Mountains and saw numerous bears one spring day. One weekend, my parents took me to Plains, Georgia, the hometown of then President Jimmy Carter. We met his mother, Lillian, at the local train depot. We saw his famous brother, Billy, at the local gas station. And, as luck would have it, we actually saw the president come out of church among a throng of reporters and camera flashes.

Those trips left a lifetime impression on me. I remember those trips with my family more than any other part of my childhood. It is not so much where we went, but that we went together as a family. Yes, my parents worked hard, sacrificed a lot, and spent many long hours away from us while working. However, they understood, and I am eternally thankful, the importance of balance and the importance of spending time together as a family.

I had a cousin who I was very close to growing up as a child. His mom and dad, my aunt and uncle, were close to my mom and dad in age, income brackets, etc. However, they never took one vacation together as a family. The dad was always gone on the weekends hunting, fishing, or pursuing other interests. The mother was always busy around the house. I would often tell my cousin about the trips we had taken, and he would always tell me that he wished his family spent time together like ours did. I felt sad for him because not only was he missing out on a rich experience, but so was his parents. I am not trying to be critical of his parents. They were good parents who provided a stable, secure home. They loved their children as much as my mom and dad loved us. However, they just lived lives that seemed to be going in different directions. Little did my aunt and uncle realize that their time together as a family would be short. In 1981, at the age of thirteen, my cousin died in a tragic motorcycle accident. Their family would never have the chance to spend a vacation together or a weekend trip together again.

One thing I love about my job is that I travel through a lot of small towns. I have the opportunity to get off the interstates and travel the rural back roads of the states I cover. It is amazing what I have seen over the years. Many times, if I have finished my calls for the day, I will drive to state parks, scenic areas, waterfalls, visit local museums, and just take in the local attractions. Along the way, I have seen the Cumberland Falls Park near Corbin, Kentucky. I have visited the birthplace of Sequoyah, the Cherokee Indian leader near Vonore, Tennessee. I have toured the Buford Pusser museum in Adamsville, Tennessee (of *"Walking Tall"* fame). I have visited the elephant sanctuary in Hohenwald, Tennessee where retired circus and zoo elephants can spend their latter years in a peaceful setting. I have visited the Cumberland Gap Park near Middlesboro, Kentucky where frontiersmen and Indians crossed the Appalachian Mountains hundreds of years ago.

I have walked down Main Street of Bristol where one side of the street is in Tennessee and the other side of the street is in Virginia. I have driven the gravel road in Butcher Hollow to where Loretta Lynn grew up in East Kentucky. I have driven through the hallowed grounds of Shiloh, Tennessee where thousands of Americans died during the civil war. I have hiked to Natural Bridge outside Lexington, Kentucky. A co-worker and I rode a ferry across Lake Erie to "Put-in-Bay," a small island just south of the Canadian border. There are so many things to see and do all around us if we will just make and take the time to discover them. Yes, work hard, but take time to observe the beauty in life. It is a chance to unwind, reflect, and refresh.

There is so much beauty, splendor, and history all around us. When we are busy, focused, and in a hurry, taking the interstate is fine. It gets you to where you need to be quickly. However, you usually do not see a lot of interesting or beautiful sites on the interstate. You have to take a detour and find the road less traveled to really see the interesting and beautiful things. Not only does this apply to traveling through Western Kentucky or East Tennessee, it applies to life as well. We need to slow down sometimes and re-kindle that child-like awe and wonder of our world. I challenge you, next time you take a trip, find a back road and see what you encounter. It may make the journey much richer and memorable.

Joseph understood the importance of balance. He knew it was crucial that he not burn out. I suspect he took time and made time to recharge and re-focus. While we should work hard and give our best while we are at work, we all need time away from our jobs to be with our families, spend time with friends, work on a hobby or passion, or just simply rest. While technology has made our jobs easier in so many ways, it is as much a curse as it is a blessing. Our addiction to smart phones, Blackberries, or I-Phones has made it virtually impossible for us to truly get away.

My father and mother-in-law live in a remote area of Colorado. Every time my wife and I go visit them, I experience a severe case of separation anxiety because there is no cell phone coverage for miles and miles. I truly have no choice but to shut the phone down and relax while we are there. For a short time, I am truly off the grid. It is amazing how great it feels to truly be unreachable for a few short days every year or so. When we finally come down from the mountain, and I boot the phone back up, I am amazed to always find the world has gone on without me. We should make an effort to put our connections to work away when we are truly on vacation.

Beginning in January of 2003, I accepted a wonderful opportunity with the company I worked for. They wanted me to move to Atlanta and manage the payment/credit card processing division for their bankcard center. It seemed like a wonderful challenge at the time. I had worked in this area for years and knew first hand that our program needed some major improvements to remain competitive in the marketplace. Our daughter was in the middle of her junior year in high school, and the bank graciously agreed to let me commute to Atlanta weekly until she graduated in May of 2004. At that time, we would re-locate permanently to Atlanta. I would usually leave Nashville on Monday, stay in Atlanta until Thursday evening, and then drive back to Nashville for the weekend.

The first few months went fine. Since I was out of town alone, I would spend countless hours at the office working on daily issues, in addition to the initiatives I was hoping to put into place. Then, I would eat dinner and go to the hotel and sit. I would become bored and pull out my laptop and work for several more hours. Then, I would get home on the weekends and find countless things I needed to follow up on. There were pricing comparisons, reports, and other tasks that I had not been able to complete while I was out of town. I would often work on these throughout the weekends, the only time at home with my wife and daughter. Around mid-year, my wife and I began to notice the arrangement was really taking a toll on our family. It was not real bad, but it was bad for us. Our daughter was going through things that teenage daughters go through, and I was not there to support my wife. I was really beginning to wonder if this arrangement would work for another year until we moved.

As fate would have it, in September of 2003, another opportunity came up in our Nashville office in a sales role. My wife and I discussed whether I should pursue it. I was concerned about the upheaval I would cause within the company if I expressed interest in the job. Management was extremely pleased with the progress we were making in the credit card area, and I feared I would be committing career suicide by changing course after just a few months. My wife and I continued to pray about it, talk about it, and think about it. In the end, I felt it was more important to preserve my family, so I pursued the role in Nashville. I was concerned that if I continued to commute to Atlanta for another year, I would put my marriage and my family under further strain.

Additionally, I was simply burned out with that job after a few short months. I had dove into the challenges of the job with such determination and gusto that I had refused to come up for air. We had made tremendous progress in implementing some much needed changes in the department, but I crashed and burned. I learned two very valuable lessons through this experience. One, I should have practiced more balance when I took the job. When I retired to the hotel for the evening, I should have left the computer off and re-charged for the next day. Second, when I came home for the weekends, I should have devoted my undivided attention to my family. A lot of people have to spend time away from their families while working. However, it is imperative that while we are at home, we focus our energy and attention on our family.

I did take the sales role in Nashville, and it worked out perfectly. When the recession hit in 2008, the bank I was working for failed. Atlanta, Georgia was ground zero for the financial meltdown in the southeast. Had we relocated to Atlanta in 2004, I am not sure what our future would have been like there. While my new job in Nashville required me to travel just as much, I learned to spend the time I had at home with my family. I started doing small things with my wife and daughter that I had not done in the past. We went to the grocery store together, we shopped together, and we went to church together. Because of this valuable lesson in balance, our marriage is more solid and richer than it has ever been.

Enjoy your work; it is a gift from God. Our work and the results of it is one of our most basic and important drivers in life. Give your work or hobby or talent its deserved time and effort, but take a break from it as well. When we balance our lives, everything seems to flow with much less resistance, and life seems to be in harmony. Joseph understood this, and God designed us for balance. Some three hundred years after Joseph's death, when Moses received the Ten Commandments from God, the fourth commandment instructed us to rest one day of the week. The purpose of the Sabbath was several fold. First and foremost, it was designed for us to pause and dwell on God and his majesty. However, the Sabbath observance was also designed for us to rest, re-boot, and refresh.

Attribute XV

Adaptability

Genesis 42:23 *They (Joseph's brothers) did not realize that Joseph could understand them, since he was using an interpreter.*

Joseph possessed the enviable and valuable ability to adapt to his surroundings. This was an amazing attribute given the time period Joseph lived in. He went from being a herder in Canaan to a slave in a metropolitan city in Egypt. He adapted quickly and rose through the ranks of authority. He was sent to prison, adapted quickly, and rose through the ranks again. He was appointed second in command of Egypt at thirty years of age and experienced tremendous success.

In this verse above, we learn that Joseph had truly adapted to the Egyptian culture in which he lived. He was dressed like an Egyptian, and he had even learned their language. Joseph recognized the world was not going to conform to him. He had to conform to the world in which he lived. He had to be flexible, adaptable, and willing to change. Once again, I point out that Joseph did not compromise his principles, morals, or faithfulness to God, but he adapted so he could be effective.

Think about how fast things are changing around us. Technological advances, global economic trends, and cultural and demographic changes within our own country are transitioning at warp speeds. To not adapt will simply mean we will be left behind. Think for just a moment how much has changed in our country in the last fifty years. When I was born in 1963, racial segregation was still common in the southeast. While I was a child, many of the major universities in the southeast admitted, very reluctantly, their first African-American students. Now, fifty years after I was born and civil rights were adopted by our country, we have an African-American president. This is nothing short of miraculous, but it also confirms that we live in a great country.

Many of our parents possibly worked for one company their entire working career. Today, Americans change jobs as often as we change air conditioner filters in our house or the oil in our cars. Our world is changing at an exponential pace. If we choose to be rigid, or are less flexible to change, we will be left in the dust.

I read a quote in Success magazine a few months ago that said, "To be a success, you must go through a constant and conscious reinvention." Never be happy with the status quo, or as I called it earlier, the "stagnation quo." If you are a creature of habit, and fear the unknown of change, start with small steps. Change some small behaviors first and de-sensitize that fear. Then, you will be able to conquer the fear of change in your life. Being receptive to change will enhance the quality of our life drastically, because it is certainly true that the only constant is change.

Joseph viewed change as an opportunity. I have learned to view change as exciting and exhilarating. Do not be frightened or intimidated by change; view change as an opportunity to experience new adventures. It is so easy to get comfortable in our environment and grow reluctant to change. But we should remember that humans, by nature, are nomadic, and in ancient times, moved and migrated to more fertile land, to where opportunities existed, so we should be open to change.

Several years ago, an engineer who worked for the company my wife works for decided to move his family to China to do mission work. He abandoned all of the comforts they knew here in the states. He left behind a secure job, a secure future, a loving extended family, and moved his family of six to China, over six thousand miles away, on the other side of the world, to conduct mission work.

In 2005, I had the privilege to travel to China and visit him, his family, and the many people he has impacted, and continues to impact, in his ministry. It was an incredible experience. He was so happy, so successful, so fulfilled, and was so confident of his purpose. His family was completely immersed in Chinese culture, language, and the entire Asian experience. He still lives there to this day, and I do not know when, or if, he will ever move back to the United States.

Joseph possessed this same attribute. Be ready and be flexible to go wherever you may be called. If we are truly willing to open ourselves to God's will in our lives, there is no telling where he may lead us. This is a frightening concept. I am not suggesting that we are all wired or geared to go overseas to do mission work. Your destiny may lie right where you are today. My destiny may be right where I am today. But we must be receptive to change in our lives.

View new technology as a friend, not a foe. Because of modern technology, I was able to record an entire album at home on a digital recorder that cost about $200. I was able to upload the album to I-tunes through a well-known website for about $50. So, for roughly $250, I had an album available to the whole world. In years past, a project like this would have cost thousands upon thousands of dollars.

Because of technology, I can write a book, upload it to a digital publisher, and sell on-demand print copies and e-copies for a few hundred bucks. In the past, this would have cost thousands of dollars. Many barriers of entry have been leveled or removed due to technology. However, those who are successful recognize that advances in technology can assist them in reaching their goals, not obstruct them from reaching their goals.

Because of modern technology, we can upload our resumes to virtually thousands of companies anywhere in the world, as opposed to reading the want ads every Sunday in the newspapers and mailing letters and resumes. Technology is great! I can assure you that Joseph utilized every tool at this disposal to achieve the successes he experienced. View change as exciting, not intimidating!

View change as an opportunity to grow, expand, and enjoy the new adventures. Great salespeople are versatile and possess a drive for continual learning. Over the years, I have attended seminars, watched webinars, read countless books, and subscribed to numerous newsletters, publications, etc., anything I can do to be better prepared and more confident in what I do. These traits and abilities do not just apply to salespeople. Housewives learn how to manage resources at home more effectively than they used to, auto mechanics have to constantly keep up with the changing technologies regarding cars and engines, and CEOs constantly have to learn new skills and management philosophies to be more effective. I read an article recently that indicated many senior executives are taking online courses in computer programming so when they approach their chief technology officers and information technology departments about technology changes, they can at least be somewhat fluent in the tech space.

Our Changing Country

Perhaps no facet of change is more prevalent than what we are seeing here in the United States. The changes in our country's demographics over the last fifty years have been astounding. Recently, I attended a banking conference and observed a presentation facilitated by Kelly McDonald from McDonald marketing. In this presentation, she discussed the changing demographics of our country. Let me share some of the facts she pointed out:

- One in three Americans are now non-white.
- Four states and the District of Columbia have "minority majority" populations, meaning that whites make up less than fifty percent of these states' population.
- The majority of our child population is non-white.
- The median age of white Americans is 41, up from 38.6 in 2000.
- Multi-racial Americans now number 8.7 million.
- The United States is the second most populous Hispanic country in the world, trailing only Mexico.
- One in six U.S. residents is Latino.
- One in four children in the U.S. is Latino.
- Married 25-34 year olds dropped from 55% in 2000 to 45% in 2010. In the 1960s, more than 80% of this age group was married.
- By 2041, white Americans will be a minority.

Yes, our country is changing rapidly. I used to hear projections like this, and it seemed so distant and unlikely. Now, we are looking at a totally different America from what our parents and grandparents experienced. The America our children and grandchildren will live in will be vastly different from our America. Many Americans view these changes with trepidation or fear. Yet, it is a reality. Our country has changed and will continue to change. We should not be scared by these statistics or trends. History has shown that races and ethnicities rise and fall in the hierarchy of relevance. It happened to the Egyptians of Joseph's day, the Persians, the Greeks, the Romans, the British, and Western Europeans. While trends and demographics may change, the God of the universe will never change. He is constant, he is steadfast, and he is there and determined to reach every man, woman, and child of every race in every remote corner of the earth.

We can view these changes negatively, or we can view these changes with much excitement and anticipation. Corporate America has caught on to our racial, ethnic, and cultural transition. I bought a new gas grill last weekend, and when I looked at the instruction booklet to see how to put it together, it was printed in seven different languages. The manufacturer of this grill has decided not to bury their head in the sand regarding changing demographics, but rather to seize the opportunity presented by a blending and transitioning culture. They have recognized it is better to be inclusive rather than exclusive.

Someone told me once to remember the five "A's" of adaptability. They are:

1. **Agility** – Be quick on your feet. Recognize the winds of change and be ready to move.
2. **Assertiveness** – Be confidant that you can change. Never develop an attitude of reluctance.
3. **Accountability** – Make your plans known to your support group. Hold yourself responsible for the ability to change.
4. **Acclimatization** – Develop and possess the ability to adjust to your surroundings quickly.

5. **Acquiescence** – Give in to change; be less resistant to new ways of doing things.

Joseph recognized that Egypt was a very different place from where he grew up. However, he chose to embrace the opportunity of diversity rather than run from it. He chose to learn their language, adapt, and integrate into their culture, while never abandoning his heritage or his faith. He recognized that for him to be effective and successful, he had to use the tools and resources at his disposal to touch lives. We have to recognize the changes that are going on in our country and learn how to touch different people in different ways. Our world, our technologies, our economies, and even our relationships go through a constant transition. We must be responsive and willing to change.

Attribute XVI

Compassion/Passion for Others

Genesis 45:1-3 *Then Joseph could no longer control himself before all his attendants, and he cried out, "Have everyone leave my presence!" So there was no one with Joseph when he made himself known to his brothers. And he wept so loudly that the Egyptians heard him, and Pharaoh's household heard about it.*

Twenty-one years had passed since Joseph's brothers had betrayed him. When he finally came face to face with them and revealed his identity, he did not act out in anger; he burst into tears. Joseph possessed compassion and passion for the very ones who sold him into slavery.

All successful people, believers and unbelievers, should possess a passion for others. To truly experience success in our lives, we must care about other people, have compassion toward other people, and possess a passion for people. The ability to help others is one of the greatest blessings that come from success.

There is no shortage of people in need. We can look in our neighborhoods, our churches, our places of employment, under the interstate bridge, or in villages and shanty towns on the other side of the world. There are millions of desperate, hurting people who need food, clothing, love, and more than anything, simply hope. We can serve and help others in endless capacities if we simply make a real effort.

Once again, I refer to Genesis 47:9, in the prison, a place where Joseph could have been consumed with self-pity and bitterness, he asked the baker and cupbearer what was troubling them. He cared enough about them to notice their countenance had changed. He had talked to them and observed them in the past, and they seemed upbeat and positive, but something was different, and Joseph noticed because he had a passion for people. By asking these two men what was troubling them, he learned of their disturbing and confusing dreams. He subsequently interpreted them, which revealed the baker would be restored and the cupbearer would meet his death. Later, even though the baker forgot to tell Pharaoh about Joseph's ability to interpret dreams for two years, he eventually told Pharaoh, and the king called for Joseph to interpret his dreams.

Had Joseph not possessed a passion for these men, he would not have noticed they were troubled. He would not have interpreted their dreams, and would not have had the opportunity to meet with Pharaoh, which led to Joseph's ultimate role in the administration. He asked about these men because he cared about them, and because of that, he was awarded with tremendous success, opportunity, and responsibility.

Successful people possess a sense of burden and an urgency to help others. They try to provide jobs, they give to charities, and they help people in their intricate circles with financial, material, and spiritual needs. Possessing a passion or compassion for others should intensify as we develop spiritual maturity because loving and serving others is a key element of the faith.

However, caring for and loving others goes much deeper than just giving to charities and causes continents away. We need to be passionate about those we come into contact with as well. We come into casual contact everyday with hundreds of people who need help. It is our responsibility to look for those opportunities and to pursue them.

I try to love everyone, but it is not always easy. The one thing I have no tolerance for is a human being mistreating another human being. Absolutely nothing stains my opinion of a person more than seeing them mistreat someone. We all have bad days, and we may take it out on someone we know, or possibly even a stranger. We must be very careful about how we treat others. We have all been in restaurants where it seems like you cannot get the waiter's attention, or you feel that you are being neglected, and we lash out at the waiter. I have been with family members, friends, customers, and associates who berate servers, cooks, hotel clerks, etc., because of perceived poor service. However, we need to take a breath before we say something we may regret. We never know what that person may be going through, and assaulting them verbally could be the last thing they need.

I believe Joseph treated every human being with dignity and respect. I think this is one of the main reasons so many thought "God was with Joseph." I sincerely believe God will place us in positions of high influence if we seize those opportunities to share encouraging words, be kind to others, and make a sincere effort to love everyone. Additionally, as we experience any level of success, I truly believed we are charged with the responsibility of caring for others. There is no shortage of needs in our neighborhoods, in our cities, in our state, in our country, or in the world.

Think of these staggering statistics our pastor shared with us several months ago:

- There are over 400 million orphans in the world today.
- 15 million children die from starvation a year, or 40,000 a day.
- 2 billion people around the world live on less than $2 a day.
- There are 27 million slaves in the world.
- There are 10 million child prostitutes in the world.

If each of us who are able would help out a little, we could change a lot in our world. We must possess a passion and a compassion for others. I truly think God will bless us with more if we are committed to helping others more. Possessing a passion for others stirs our motivation and incents us to achieve more.

Our pastor has spoken on this topic a lot lately, and it is very stirring. He has stated often that "indifference is a curse." We cannot allow our conscience to harden to the needs of others. It is easy to sweep concern under the rug and to block out the obvious needs that surround us. However, I truly think God will confront us when we face him if we have not made some real effort to help those in need.

When we develop and establish our life goals, the enhancement and improvement of mankind should be a key and integral part of this strategy. We must possess a passion, compassion, and empathy for those who are suffering or in need. Some fifteen hundred years after Joseph, after Jesus was crucified and ascended to heaven, the early Christian Church was very focused on helping those in need. Many churches still help those in need, but we must personally be committed to helping those in need.

Likewise, we should develop a passion for causes that mean something to us. Our daughter, who is twenty-six now, seemed to struggle for some time because she did not feel she really possessed a passion for anything specific. However, after graduating college a few years ago and getting her first apartment, she decided she wanted a small dog. She began to research animal rescues. She was appalled at how poorly dogs are treated in a lot of breeding situations. She was shocked to learn that some breeders would use dogs until they were too old to breed, and then they would discard the animals at shelters or on the side of the road. The proliferation in cases of animal abuse, especially in the southeast, has caused her to develop a passion for animals and rescues. I can honestly say that I have never seen her so passionate about anything. Now, she is constantly looking for ways to help rescues, often volunteering her time to clean kennels, bathe animals, or whatever she can do to help these poor animals. She attempts to educate others on the conditions of these breeding operations and urges others to adopt from shelters because there is such an abundance of need. When you develop a passion for something, it drives you to achieve extraordinary goals. Your passion may be animals, the homeless, people with addictions, veterans returning from war with post traumatic issues, or any number of social issues. Develop a passion for a cause and you develop purpose in your life.

Attribute XVII

Forgiveness

Genesis 45:4-12 *"So then, it was not you who sent me here, but God. He made me father to Pharaoh, lord of his entire household and ruler of all Egypt. Now hurry back to my father and say to him, this is what your son Joseph says: God has made me Lord of all Egypt. Come down to me; don't delay. You shall live in the region of Goshen and be near to me-you your children and grandchildren, your flocks and herds, and all you have. I will provide for you there, because five years of famine are still to come. Otherwise you and your household and all who belong to you will become destitute."*

We have all been wronged, cheated, shorted, or betrayed by someone in our lives. We have all wronged, cheated, shorted, or betrayed someone in our lives. Forgiving others is crucial to experiencing fulfilling success in our lives. We must learn to move past wrongs in our lives. Joseph recognized the power and freedom that results from forgiveness.

Joseph experienced the ultimate in betrayal. Joseph had the authority, the capacity, and the opportunity to exert revenge on his brothers. However, when Joseph came face to face with the very brothers who conspired initially to kill him, but then sold him to the slave traders, he did not seek revenge. Rather, Joseph experienced tremendous grief when he finally encountered his brothers. Joseph understood that bitterness and anger would undermine and erode his focus on success. He chose, as difficult as it must have been, not to dwell on the past. He focused on the present and the potential of the future.

It is human nature to be angry and to hold grudges against those who have wronged us. However, we must keep in mind, and for me especially, that I have wronged others as well. As much as I need to forgive others, I need others to forgive me. Maybe not to the degree of betrayal that Joseph's brothers committed, but I have certainly wronged others.

Once again, Joseph understood God's sovereignty in his life. He understood that if his brothers had not betrayed him, he never would have ended up in Egypt. Had he not ended up in Egypt, he never would have ended up in Potiphar's house. If he had not ended up in Potiphar's house, he would not have ended up in the Egyptian prison. If he had not ended up in prison, he never would have had the opportunity to address Pharaoh and serve under him. He also understood that if these events had not occurred as they did, he would not have been in a position to save the entire region from famine. Joseph simply accepted his circumstances. He never harbored jealousy or bitterness. He simply pursued God and trusted that all would work out in the end.

But equally as important as knowing God's sovereignty, Joseph also possessed an understanding of God's nature. Joseph knew, because of his spiritual maturity, that God forgives us for many betrayals, and he understood that forgiveness is crucial to experiencing true success, fulfillment, and purpose. Had Joseph been bitter toward his brothers and had he been focused only on getting revenge, his other attributes would have been neutralized or weakened. Think about it, if you are consumed with anger, rage, and bitterness toward someone who has wronged you, your integrity will be challenged, you will not be content, your motivations will deviate from their correct course, you will most certainly not be likable, and your critical thinking skills will be skewed, and so on.

Joseph understood that for him to be a true representation of God, and for him to stand out in the crowd, he had to move on and focus on the tasks at hand. Joseph did not mope around dwelling on the past and crying "woe is me." He recognized that he had a platform and an opportunity to glorify God, and he concentrated on that.

Bitterness Corrupts Potential

Harboring resentment and anger toward those who have wronged us will only corrupt our ultimate potential. It serves as a distraction from what we should be focusing on. Satan has achieved much success against mankind by instilling anger, bitterness, and revenge in our hearts.

I recently watched the new production of the Hatfields and McCoys on the History Channel. I watched in amazement as these two families fought, injured, and killed each other over the course of several decades in what began in large part as a dispute over a pig. Nothing of significance can be accomplished through revenge or retaliation against someone who has wronged us. Had Joseph chose to allow bitterness to consume him, he would have floundered, failed, and never achieved what God had in store for him. He recognized that it was his responsibility to create something positive out of a horrible betrayal.

In July of 1997, a first cousin of mine was brutally murdered in Chattanooga, Tennessee. "Marty" Davis was a well respected Episcopalian priest. He was a pillar of the community, and he possessed a tremendous passion to serve the inner city needs of the area. The local news media would often run stories about how Marty was helping the homeless and needy in the Chattanooga area. Police believe a man went to Marty's house to either borrow money or to rob him. Whatever the motive, the confrontation became violent, and the man shot Marty several times at point blank range. To this day, the perpetrator has never been apprehended, and the crime remains one of Chattanooga's darkest cold cases.

A day or two after the murder, a memorial service was held at the church where Marty served. A reporter from one of the local television stations was interviewing Marty's brother, Tommy. The reporter asked Tommy what he would like to see happen to the murderer of his younger brother. In one of the most amazing acts of forgiveness I have ever seen, Marty's brother simply said, "I would like to see this person accept Jesus Christ as his savior." I almost burst into tears when I heard Tommy's response. What an amazing display of constraint, compassion, and forgiveness.

I hope I will never have to forgive someone for something so violent, senseless, and callous. I can only hope that I will forgive those who wrong or have wronged me in the past and in the future. Just as important, I hope that others will forgive me for the wrongs I have committed. I cannot erase the wrongs I have committed in the past, but I can certainly work toward not wronging others in the future. Joseph knew that anger and bitterness would distract him from fulfilling his purpose, potential, and his ultimate success. He also knew that harboring resentment would distract him from glorifying God, his chief purpose. He chose to turn the betrayal by his brothers over to God and allow him to work it out in his time, in his wisdom, and his way.

Seeking Forgiveness

As equally important as giving, forgiving is seeking forgiveness. It is a humbling and gratifying experience to sincerely ask someone for forgiveness. However, we must realize that we make mistakes and hurt people as well. I can remember countless times in my life where I wronged someone, treated someone badly, or found myself being selfish in a relationship. I have apologized to those when the opportunity has arisen, and I have sought God's forgiveness as well.

One of the most compelling stories in recent political history involved the relationship between Michael Dukakis and Lee Atwater. As you may remember, Michael Dukakis was the 1988 Democratic presidential nominee. Lee Atwater was an up-and-coming young Republican strategist working for the George H. Bush ticket. Dukakis emerged from the 1988 Democratic convention with a seemingly insurmountable 18 point lead in the polls over George H. Bush, the Republican presidential nominee who had served two terms as vice president under Ronald Reagan.

Just when it appeared that the Bush campaign would lose, Lee Atwater and other Republican strategists came up with a brilliant plan that would alter the outcome of the election. Somehow, Atwater discovered that during Dukakis' stint as Governor of Massachusetts, he had endorsed a prison furlough program. As a result of this furlough program, a convicted felon named Willie Horton was released from prison for a weekend. Sadly, Willie Horton abducted, raped, and murdered a woman during this furlough. Atwater and the Republicans began bombarding the airwaves with searing political ads painting Dukakis as a New England liberal who was soft on crime. Democratic leaders cried foul and suggested the ads were racially insulting (Horton was black). I still remember the frightening and menacing picture of Horton in the ads on television.

Whether the ads were fair or not, they worked. Bush began to surge in the polls, Dukakis never recovered, and Bush went on to trounce Dukakis in one of the biggest comebacks in American political history. As often happens, Michael Dukakis, the loser, drifted into obscurity after the election, and Atwater became a darling of the Republican Party. His future seemed extremely bright, and tremendous potential lie ahead.

Coincidentally, in 1990, just two years after the election, Lee Atwater was diagnosed with a terminal brain tumor and given just a few months to live. In an instant, at forty years old, Lee Atwater went from having an unlimited future to making plans for his final days, weeks, and maybe months. As often happens when we are facing death, Atwater turned to faith and became a practicing Catholic. Lee Atwater began to evaluate his life and how he wanted to spend his last few months. He realized it was important to apologize to those he had hurt in his life. As a result, he began to feel a deep burden to make amends with Michael Dukakis. He also felt a burden to apologize to his counterpart at the Democratic Party, Ron Brown, the Democratic Party Chairman. Atwater and Brown had a contentious relationship as chairmen of the opposing political parties. Brown would later serve as Bill Clinton's Commerce Secretary until he died tragically in a plane crash.

Atwater mailed Michael Dukakis a letter explaining his situation and asked for forgiveness. Dukakis accepted his apology and forgave Atwater for his trespasses. Atwater also apologized to Ron Brown, the DNC chairperson. Atwater would later write that he was often rude to Brown and intentionally avoided him in public. However, before Atwater died, Ron Brown, his Democratic adversary, became a close friend and spent much time with Lee and his wife in the weeks preceding Lee's death. This story reminds us that our priorities today may not be our priorities tomorrow. It also reveals that when we are facing mortality, we really long for forgiveness, to give it and to receive it. In an article for Life magazine in November of 1991, shortly before he died, Lee Atwater stated the following:

"My illness helped me to see that what was missing in society is what was missing in me: a little heart, a lot of brotherhood. The 80s were about acquiring — acquiring wealth, power, and prestige. I know. I acquired more wealth, power, and prestige than most. But you can acquire all you want and still feel empty. What power wouldn't I trade for a little more time with my family? What price wouldn't I pay for an evening with friends? It took a deadly illness to put me eye to eye with that truth, but it is a truth that the country, caught up in its ruthless ambitions and moral decay, can learn on my dime. I don't know who will lead us through the 90s, but they must be made to speak to this spiritual vacuum at the heart of American society, this tumor of the soul."

It is evident in scripture that Joseph's brothers desperately sought his forgiveness. I sense based on the emotional response of his brothers that this act of betrayal had haunted them for years. I do not believe for a moment that the brothers were contrite just because they needed food from him when they came face to face with him in Egypt. I suspect guilt and remorse plagued their entire lives until they were able to reconcile with Joseph.

The Most Important Person to Forgive

It is certainly important that we forgive those who have wronged us. Nothing can be gained from holding bitter grudges toward others. It is also important that we seek forgiveness from those we have wronged. It is up to them as to whether they forgive you, but at least you will have acknowledged your wrongs. It is also important in our faith walk that we regularly seek forgiveness from God for our sins.

But equally as important as these, we must also forgive ourselves. We have all made mistakes, missed opportunities, and done things we wish we could undo. I have certainly made my share of mistakes in life. I would give anything to have done some things differently. However, the past is the past, and we cannot re-live it. If God, or others, is willing to forgive us for our past mistakes, we certainly must be willing to forgive ourselves. We are only robbing ourselves of precious time, resources, and emotions when we constantly re-hash the past and re-live our mistakes.

Yes, we must evaluate our errors. We should dissect our failures to see what led to the mistake. We should resolve to not make those same mistakes again. But after that, we have to let it go, chalk it up to experience, and move on. Constantly feeding on past mistakes will create a perpetual, emotional wound that never heals. It may scab over, but we scrape the scab off and it bleeds again and again. When God forgives us for a sin, we must forgive ourselves and move on.

Attribute XVIII

Meaningful Relationships

Genesis 45:14-15 *Then he threw his arms around Benjamin and wept, and Benjamin embraced him, weeping. And he kissed all his brothers and wept over them. Afterward his brothers talked with him.*

It is evident from Joseph's life that he valued meaningful relationships. He was close to his father when he was young. He formed deep relationships with people he encountered throughout his life. Later, after marrying, Joseph and his wife had two children, and he experienced complete success and fulfillment because he understood the value of meaningful relationships.

Success can be a wonderful experience. However, we need meaningful relationships in our lives to experience total completeness. Success without people to love, or to be loved, can be a hollow experience. This does not imply that single people cannot experience success, fulfillment, and purpose. However, everyone longs for people to love, share with, and have communion with.

I was a teenager in the late 1970s. One of my favorite rock bands was Boston. This group burst onto the music scene in the mid-seventies with their unique vocals, searing guitar riffs, and a special sound that became a staple of the "FM rock" era. Their debut album sold twenty-six million copies. Brad Delp was the original lead singer and one of the founders of the band. The band had numerous hits, sold millions of records, filled stadiums with screaming fans, and experienced tremendous success. While sounds, styles, and trends changed as they always do, Boston was always a recognizable sound that I loved to listen to, and still do to this day.

In 2007, I was saddened to learn that Brad Delp had committed suicide. Apparently he had battled depression for a period of time and concluded life was not worth living. According to authorities, he lit two charcoal grills in the bathroom of his New Hampshire home, laid down in the floor with his head on a pillow, and succumbed to carbon monoxide poisoning. When police arrived and discovered him, they found a note that read: "Mr. Brad Delp. Ja'ai une ame solitaire. I am a lonely soul."

I do not know all of the circumstances surrounding the issues in his life, but the point is this. Volumes could be written regarding people throughout history who seemed to have it all, only to discover they suffered from the worst curse possible, isolation and loneliness. Having people in our lives that we love and that love us is crucial to experiencing total success and happiness. Life can seem very empty and dark without people to love and to be loved by.

Space

While interaction with those we have relationships with is crucial, we must also recognize that we need space from others, and they need space for themselves. We lead hectic lives; our schedules are exhausting, consuming, and tiring. At times, we all need to back up, relax, and spend some time alone. We need to "defrag," unwind, and chill out. Those we love also need time for themselves. We should make a concerted effort to take a day or two here and there to spend alone, focusing on our goals, our accomplishments, and our shortcomings.

We need time to reflect, recharge, refresh our minds, re-evaluate our positioning, and re-align our lives with God. While we can do this through Church and small groups, we need time alone. Our spouses need time alone as well. As a man, I realize that my wife is chained to our home much more than I am. I can travel, be gone a few days, and mow the grass when I get home. She does not have the luxury of escape. She comes home every day at lunch, lets the dogs out, washes the laundry, mails the bills, balances the checkbook, washes more laundry, and on and on.

She never complains or backs off, however, sometimes, she will just go get a manicure, or a pedicure, or go for a massage. I encourage her to do this. We all need our down time.

I suspect Joseph spent a lot of time reflecting on his life, his goals, his efforts, and his relationship with God. I think it was easier then because there were fewer distractions. Regardless, we must make time to be alone. God yearns for our attention. Spending time alone allows us the time we need to develop that deeper relationship with God we need to be more successful.

Additionally, we need to develop hobbies and pastimes. I love music. I have played piano since I was a child. I enjoy going in my music room and playing guitar or piano. That is an escape for me. I also like to play golf, as frustrating as it can be. I enjoy reading and writing. It serves as an escape and a form of relaxation. If you do not have a hobby or pastime, I encourage you to explore and discover something that you have a passion for and enjoy doing. God did not intend for life to be a constant grind for us. He wants us to enjoy life along the way. We do that by finding things that exhilarate and inspire us. I assure you that Joseph had hobbies and pastimes he enjoyed.

Circles of Influence – Who We Surround Ourselves With

In addition to having meaningful relationships with family, we need to be intentional regarding the people we have around us. Joseph did not surround himself with people who would bring him down emotionally, spiritually, morally, or through destructive attitudes. When his father asked him to check on his brothers, Joseph was at home where he was likely experiencing positive reinforcement. He was not hanging out with his brothers, who were negative, cynical, or critical. This may have been due to his responsibilities around the home, or Joseph may have realized that being around them would be a negative experience.

I suspect that while Joseph worked for Potiphar, he chose to surround himself with people who would encourage, enlighten, and share wisdom with him about his future. He did not hang around with the other servants who likely complained and whined about their circumstances.

Research has proven that we tend to emulate those we hang around with. If we hang around losers, negative thinkers, or disrupters of progress, we will think like they do. This does not mean that we do not try to touch, influence, encourage, or change these types of people. It simply means that we will mirror, admire, and pursue the course of action of those we surround ourselves with. With that being said, we need to be around successful people to improve our likelihood of success. We need to observe and imitate those who have experienced fulfillment and purpose in their lives. We should try to reflect the behavior of those we admire in our lives.

Likewise, we should flee those who tear us down, avoid those who have a "misery loves company" attitude, and stay away from people who may influence us in a negative way. However, while we need to surround ourselves with positive, successful people, we should still possess a passion and desire to change the course of those who are charting a different or destructive path.

When my dad owned a car business, he had a lot of guys who worked for him who made pretty good money, considering their skills, education, and abilities. However, many of them practiced a very destructive pattern of lifestyle that included alcohol abuse, drug abuse, gambling, poor financial management skills, and life skills that made life more difficult than it should have or could have been. I observed at a young age that those people influenced each other very much. They tended to emulate the practices of each other. I saw guys draw $1,000 paychecks on Friday evenings, and by Monday morning, they were flat broke. Often they chose to go out to the bars, drink, chase women, gamble, do drugs, or practice poor decision-making choices.

Most of these guys lived in a perpetual trap of owing, borrowing, and literally surviving week to week. In reality, had they practiced some solid money management skills, they could have made a decent living and improved their lifestyles substantially. Sadly, these behaviors seem to be passed from generation to generation. Likewise, wise decision making skills seem to be passed on from generation to generation.

Additionally, I observed others who seemed to achieve success. They practice different principles in all aspects of their lives than those who do not achieve success. Is that coincidental?

I do not think so. I realized, thankfully, that if I wanted to be a failure, I only needed to surround myself with failing people. If I wanted to be a success, I needed to surround myself with successful people.

This is a simple principle. If you are constantly around those who fail, choose to fail, and do not care if they fail, you will inevitably fall into that pattern of behavior. If you want to achieve extraordinary results, you need to surround yourself with extraordinary people. This does not imply that we need to abandon destructive people; quite the contrary. We need to embrace them, encourage them, and lead them to a more productive life. However, we do not achieve that by following their behavior. We do that by setting an example.

Encourage and Support Those We Love

It is imperative that we encourage, challenge, and support those in our lives. This is especially true regarding our family members. People love to be acknowledged, recognized, and encouraged. This is especially true regarding our children. We must constantly give them positive feedback and appreciation for a job well done, and fair and constructive criticism when they fall short on expectations. I have seen so many parents who constantly belittle and criticize their children every time they make a mistake.

Lead by Example

It is absurd to criticize our children or others for falling short on goals and accomplishments if we are not leading by example. Our children will generally emulate the behaviors of their parents. If our children observe us being successful, hard working, caring, and loving, they are much more likely to follow in our steps. I am reminded of the story where a father, disappointed at his son's lack of motivation, said, "When Abraham Lincoln was your age, he walked a mile in the snow each way to school every day. When he returned home in the afternoon, he would cut wood for the fireplace before dinner." The son looked at his dad and said, "When Abraham Lincoln was your age, he was president of the United States!" Be cautious when criticizing those you love. If criticism is necessary, do so in a loving, respectful tone. Always take a careful look in the mirror before you point out their weaknesses.

Joseph obviously understood the value and the place relationships held in his life. He loved his father, despite mistakes and shortcomings Jacob had in his life. Joseph loved his brothers, despite the fact they betrayed him, gave serious thought to killing him, and ultimately sold him into slavery. He loved those he worked with and worked for. When he married and had children, he was a loving husband and father. To be truly successful, fulfilled, and to live out our purpose, we must have people we love in every stage of our lives.

Relationship Killers

I read an interesting article recently written by a gentleman by the name of Dr. John Gottman. He is the lead researcher for the Gottman Institute at Seattle University in Seattle, Washington. In this article, the doctor listed four behaviors that almost always destroy marriages. However, I think this can be applied to any relationship, regardless of how strong they may be. These included:

- **Constant criticism** – When we constantly criticize someone for things they do, do not do, should have done, or should not have done, it will always create animosity and resentment. Eventually, the person who is constantly criticized will throw up their hands in frustration or throw in the towel on the marriage or relationship. Eventually, they may come to hate you.

- **Contempt** – This is when someone constantly and intentionally insults someone. Often, this may begin as criticism and turn into contempt. Contempt can be committed verbally, physically, or through body language. Continual contempt will eventually poison a relationship.

- **Defensiveness** – This involves sidestepping responsibilities or reacting negatively to fair criticism. Sometimes,
  fair and constructive criticism is a good thing. React
  positively to constructive criticism and make an effort to
  change what is undermining your relationship.

- **Stonewalling** – This also includes withdrawing, which
  men are notorious for when faced with criticism from a
  spouse or friend. We must be transparent, accessible, and
  interested in constructive dialogue.

If you seem to have trouble establishing, retaining, and
strengthening relationships in your life, whether they are roman-
tic, plutonic, or family relationships, evaluate your behavior in
these relationships and ensure you are not guilty of these traps. In
the end, relationships require trust, respect, honestly, and
sacrifice. It is imperative that we have people in our lives that we
love and that love us. Life is just easier with meaningful
relationships.

Never Take a Day for Granted

It was Thanksgiving day, 1987. I was twenty-four years old and
still single at the time. A best friend of mine had spent the
Wednesday night before thanksgiving at the apartment I shared
with a friend. We had passed the Wednesday evening by playing
cards and listening to music. On Thanksgiving morning, I was
driving him out to his mother's house for an early Thanksgiving
lunch/dinner. It was a cold, clear November morning, and a milky
frost covered the barren fields. We were driving along, enjoying
the serenity of the morning, when abruptly, we topped a small hill
and saw a young teenage boy running down the road. He was
obviously scared, looked pale, and seemed to be in shock. I
looked at Jim, and we both realized something was dreadfully
wrong. We pulled over to the side of the road and rolled down the
driver's side window. I asked, "What's wrong?"

The young boy replied, "I just shot my cousin!"

Jim and I looked at each other with dread. Out of instinct, I
punched the accelerator and cruised over the small hill. Sure

enough, lying in the road, was a young teenage boy. I stopped the
vehicle, and Jim and I jumped out of the car. By that time, the
cousin had caught up with us. It was apparently clear that this was
a very grave situation.

Jim and I knew immediately that the injuries were likely
fatal. Although he was not dead, he was not conscious; although
we tried to get his attention, he was unresponsive. After a few
minutes, Jim recommended that I drive down the road, find a
house, and have someone call an ambulance. Keep in mind, this
was years before cell phones.

Jim recommended that I take the distraught teenager with me
to divert him from the trauma of the scene and the situation. The
boy and I jumped in the car and drove down the road to the first
house we saw. We screeched to a stop, I jumped out of the car,
and ran to the door. I knocked, and after a brief eternity, an
elderly woman opened the door, oblivious to the severity of the
situation. I asked the woman to call the sheriff's department and
an ambulance as soon as possible.

The young boy and I drove back to the scene of the accident.
Jim was trying to administer basic first aid treatment to the
victim, but I sensed from the look on his face that the boy's
condition was deteriorating. We kept waiting. Everything seemed
like a blur. After a few minutes, a couple of vehicles arrived, and
we realized this was the immediate family members of the victim
and the kid who accidentally shot him. These family members
jumped from the vehicles and immediately and understandably
burst into an emotional outcry of despair and shock. Jim and I
stood by helplessly, assuring the family members that help would
arrive soon.

After what seemed like an eternity, we heard the wailing
sound of the sirens in the distance. Finally, the sheriff's department and ambulance service arrived. They immediately kicked in
to emergency mode and provided every effort available at that
time to save the young boy's life.

The deputies asked me and Jim a few cursory questions
about the incident, asked for our phone numbers in case there
were any questions, and in a wisp, everyone disappeared. The
ambulance was gone, the deputies were gone, and the families
were gone.

We drove on to Jim's mom's house for Thanksgiving. By the time I went to my mom and dad's that evening, word had gotten around town that the young boy had in fact passed away. His cousin had shot him at close range accidentally in a freak accident. One moment these two families were preparing for a joyful holiday together, but within a few hours, they were preparing for a funeral. Every Thanksgiving I think about those families and what happened over twenty years ago.

The reason I tell this story is this. We never know when our lives are going to be thrown into upheaval. Tragedy can strike at anytime, anyplace. If you have teenagers or young adult children, you know the worries and fears of being a parent. We should embrace, cherish, and relish every good moment we have with our families and friends. In a blink of an eye, everything can change.

Heaven forbid we should ever go through anything like these families went through. But the worst thing that could happen would be to look back after a tragedy and realize that we did not share in the happiness that was ours before. We should hug the ones we love, tell the ones we love that we love them every day, and be grateful for the precious present with those we love.

Friends for a Season

Sometimes God sends special people into our lives for a reason, and perhaps just for a season. I remember when my dad was sick, I had just met a new co-worker named Rob. He was a great guy, and we hit it off immediately. He became my best friend, aside from my wife, during this difficult time. When I was depressed, he cheered me up. When I was sad, he would do things to take my mind off what was bothering me. We went trout fishing; we went to NASCAR races. He was there during a difficult time. He helped our family move to Nashville, and although we stay in touch occasionally, we are not as close as we were during that time.

During that same period, my wife became great friends with a lady named Beth. They would walk together, make crafts together, and talk a lot. Just so happens that Beth's husband had lost his dad to a sickness a few years before we went through this.

Beth was able to share insights into how she comforted her husband during that difficult time. Even though they have stayed in touch over the years, they are not as close as they were during that season. God understands that sometimes we need different people in our lives, people with different experiences and perspectives, to help us through a situation. I am sure Joseph had these relationships as well. Recognize them, appreciate them, and thank God for sending these folks into our lives.

Attribute XIX

Sacrifice

Genesis 47:11-12 *So Joseph settled his father and his brothers in Egypt and gave them property in the best part of the land, the district of Ramses, as Pharaoh directed, Joseph also provided his father and his brothers and all his father's household with food, according to the number of their children.*

Once reunited with his family, Joseph sacrificed for them and gave them the best land in the region. Success will always require sacrifice. To accomplish anything of any value, it will require sacrifice. If something is so easy to obtain that it does not require sacrifice, then it is likely not worth pursuing. You can evaluate the habits, traits, practices, and skills of anyone in any walk of life, and you will always see a consistent trail of sacrifice. To have a meaningful relationship with God, we must sacrifice. To have a successful marriage or human relationship, we must sacrifice. To accomplish great things or to receive promotions at work, we must sacrifice.

The super athletes we admire for their strength, agility, success, and wealth are where they are because they learned at a young age they had to sacrifice. They got up early while their friends were still sleeping in to work out or practice. They avoided and missed out on certain things that the average person was not willing to miss out on so they could achieve success. A success-driven person understands that success does not come easy. They understand success is not going to be handed to them.

The best way to have the best shot at success comes through sacrifice.

Additionally, not only are success-driven people willing to sacrifice so they can achieve great things, they are also willing to sacrifice so that those in their lives may have a better life. My parents worked hard and sacrificed so they could succeed. They also worked hard and sacrificed so that I would have a better chance than they did at succeeding. They did not want my brother and I to have to do some of the things they were willing to do in the future. This is a noble pursuit for which I am eternally grateful. Most parents understand this aspect of sacrifice. My wife and I worked hard and saved so our daughter could go to college without taking on student debt. We wanted her, when she graduated, to have a better start than we had. I am certain in her time, when and if she has children, she will want her children to have even better opportunities than she had.

Between 1989 and 1991, I worked the third shift at American National Bank in Chattanooga, Tennessee sorting checks. There was an elderly African-American man, probably in his late seventies, who cleaned up the building during the overnight hours. He was a pleasant and humble man who had a constant smile and was always willing to chat for a few minutes. Late one night, he told me that he worked third shift at the bank, then worked as a daytime janitor at another business. I was surprised that he was working two jobs at his age. He told me he was doing this so he could put all of his grandchildren through college. He had already put three through college and had two more to go. Then, he said with a smile, he would retire. He was always excited and ready to brag on how well his grandchildren were doing and how proud he was of them. He told me that he wanted his grandchildren to have better opportunities than he had. That is sacrifice.

As a child, I remember my father leaving for work before daylight on many mornings and often not getting home until ten or eleven o'clock at night. I remember his knuckles and fingers would be bleeding from where he had cut them working under the hood of a car. Once, he had a car radiator blow up in his face and had to be rushed to the emergency room with scalding burns on his face. I remember him hauling cars and breaking down on the side of deserted interstates at night, way before cell phones were common, and then walking to an exit to call for help. He did all of these things so he could have a better life than his parents had, and so that we could have a better life than he had. This is sacrifice.

I had several great uncles who joined the military in World War II, left their wives and children behind for years, and fought on foreign soil that they had never even heard of. Some of them returned with physical and emotional wounds that haunted them for the rest of their lives. They did this to liberate and free people who were under the oppression of sadistic leaders. They did this so that their children and their grandchildren could live in a country that was free, and so that their children and grandchildren could have better opportunities than they had. This is sacrifice.

Joseph was willing to sacrifice. He pursued perfection and success through sacrifice. He was willing to give up what others were not willing to give up so that when God placed opportunities in front of him, he was prepared to succeed. Talk to anyone who has ever succeeded at any endeavor, and they will tell you it required sacrifice.

Around 6:30 AM on January 2, 2006, an explosion occurred deep within a coal mine in Sago, West Virginia. It is widely believed the explosion was caused when lightening from a passing thunderstorm struck the mountain and ignited a pocket of explosive methane gas. Just a few minutes before the explosion blocked the tunnel leading to and from the mine, thirteen miners had just entered the mountain to begin their shift for the day. After attempting to exit the mine, only to find the entrance blocked by rock and deadly, acrid smoke, the miners retreated deep inside the mine and followed the safety protocol they had been trained to exercise. First, they erected a plastic sheet to serve as a curtain to hopefully block the deadly carbon monoxide from enveloping them. Next, they activated the small canisters of emergency oxygen that was given to each miner. Within these small canisters was enough oxygen to last only an hour or two at the most for each miner. Next, all they could do was wait and hope that rescuers could make it to them in time.

The entire nation watched anxiously as rescuers desperately and frantically attempted to get to the miners in time. Hour after painful hour slipped by, and experts and pundits alike espoused opinions as to how long they could survive and what their condition would be if they were located. It would be forty-one torturous hours later on January 4 before rescuers broke through the rock and debris and located the miners. After much confusion and miscommunication to the families and the media about the number of survivors and their conditions, the somber announcement was made that only one of the miners had survived.

Randal L. McCloy Jr., age twenty-six at the time, was the only miner who survived the disaster. He was rushed to a hospital in nearby Charleston, West Virginia where emergency treatment for acute carbon monoxide poisoning was administered. After several months of treatment and rehabilitation, Randal recovered. In April of 2006, McCloy wrote a letter to the immediate family members of the miners who had died in the tragedy. He detailed how the miners attempted to exit the shaft only to find the exit obstructed and filled with toxic fumes. They retreated deep within the bowels of the mine and erected the curtain. Then, McCloy told that some of the emergency respirators were not working. He went on to explain that the miners who had functioning respirators shared theirs with the others. Although the miners knew this limited amount of precious oxygen was all they had to sustain them until help arrived, they willingly sacrificed their oxygen with the other miners in an effort to save each other. Eventually, McCloy went to explain, the miners came to the stark realization that help would not likely arrive in time to save them. The miners gathered together and prayed the "miner's prayer." Some wrote notes to their loved ones, which were given to their families later, and they began to drift off into unconsciousness.

I cannot begin to comprehend what these men must have felt when they realized it was likely they would die in the mine. The most touching aspect of this sad story was how the miners shared their oxygen with each other. What a tremendous display of sacrifice. I am not surprised these gentlemen shared their oxygen. When you are involved in something with others you care about, share a common bond with, and love, you are willing to sacrifice without a second thought. These men had worked together for years and were willing to sacrifice the very air they breathed for a chance at saving the group as a whole.

Joseph understood sacrifice is a key precept of faith and love. Some fifteen hundred years after Joseph died, God would provide the ultimate display of sacrifice when he sent Jesus to this earth to be scorned, rejected, and put to death by the very people he came to save.

A few years ago, some bankers, including myself, had the privilege of attending a dinner at the home of a well respected, very successful country music producer and songwriter in Nashville. This man has been behind some of the biggest hits and country music artists in Nashville over the last thirty years. As an amateur musician and a life-long lover of country music, I was captivated as he told us stories of the entertainers he had worked with, the songs he had written and produced, and stories of the industry in general. I was in awe as he and his wife gave us a tour of their opulent home, and I stared in admiration at the gold and platinum albums and records he had on display like trophies.

At some point during the night, his wife mentioned that they often visit with aspiring writers, producers, arrangers, etc. Usually these discussions involve guidance, wisdom, and tips on how to survive the unpredictable, topsy-turvy world of the music business. Most of these aspiring artists, in their naïve understanding of the business, are expecting an easy shortcut to success in the grueling music business. She mentioned that she often tells the wives or husbands in some cases, to prepare for years of poverty, denial, cheap dinners at fast food restaurants, or sometimes even going hungry. She added that she would tell them that if they were very lucky, perhaps one day they could actually make a living in the business. She told us how she shared this reality with those folks so they would know how truly hard it is to make it in the business.

The wife went on to tell us how when they first moved to Nashville years ago, with nothing in tow but their dreams, she would often cut coupons out of the local newspapers for meals at local restaurants, she would buy food in mass quantities at discount grocers because they had little income, and how they both sacrificed for the dreams they sought. She laughed as she told of countless aspiring singers, writers, and producers who had come to them for counsel and was shocked and appalled when they learned how much this family had sacrificed before they experienced success. These aspiring hopefuls were surprised to learn the road to success would have to be paved with hard work, sacrifice, uncertainty, and pain.

In the end, this couple succeeded and enjoyed the fruits of their labor together because they both understood that achieving their dreams would not be easy and would require sacrifice. Yes, they live the dream life now, but this couple understood that sacrifice would be required to achieve their dreams and desires. More importantly, they were in it together.

Joseph understood this as well. Make no mistake, whatever your goal in life may be, achieving it will not always be easy. Even if you possess tremendous gifts, nothing comes easy. Sacrifice will always be required. Success will taste sweeter and success will be more appreciated if sacrifice is required. Relationships are deeper and stronger when sacrifice is required.

Attribute XX

Loyalty

Genesis 50:22-26 *Joseph stayed in Egypt, along with his entire father's family. He lived a hundred and ten years and saw the third generation of Ephraim's children. Also the children of Makir son of Manasseh were placed on Joseph's knees. The Joseph said to his brothers, "I am about to die. But God will surely come to your aid and take you up out of this land to the land he promised on oath to Abraham, Isaac, and Jacob." And Joseph made the sons of Israel swear an oath and said, "God will surely come to your aid, and then you must carry my bones up from this place." So Joseph died at the age of a hundred and ten. And after they embalmed him, he was placed in a coffin in Egypt.*

The final attribute of Joseph we explore is loyalty. Of all the attributes, I fear that loyalty may be the most endangered in our society. When I first entered the work force, it was not uncommon to see people work for the same organization their entire career. Now, college graduates can expect to work for fifteen different companies throughout their career. This in itself is not bad, as we should be adaptable and flexible and enjoy new experiences and take advantage of better opportunities. However, we should not abandon loyalty.

Joseph recognized the importance of loyalty. This was a major key to his success. While he worked for Potiphar, he was loyal to Potiphar. When he worked for Pharaoh, he was loyal to Pharaoh. Likewise, Potiphar and Pharaoh were loyal to Joseph.

While I do not necessarily believe in "karma," I will say that with loyalty, you get back what you give. I truly believe if you are loyal to others, they will be loyal to you. Joseph was loyal to God. No matter where he ended up, no matter how he got there, he never abandoned God. Even though he integrated into Egyptian culture and took on their customs and language, he was still loyal to God. Even though he had allegiances to Pharaoh, he was loyal to his family when they came to him. Joseph was loyal to his heritage. Joseph asked that his bones be returned to the land of his father's when he died, and several hundred years later, this request was honored.

Pharaoh presented Joseph with the signet ring and robe to prove his loyalty. Joseph did not have to be distracted by wondering if Pharaoh was loyal to him. Joseph headed up the famine initiative with great success because he knew Pharaoh had his back. Everything seems to work in harmony when loyalty is in place. Marriages, romances, relationships with siblings, parents, and children flow in harmony when loyalty is obvious.

Consider this. Joseph likely accumulated a considerable amount of wealth while working for the King of Egypt. Once the famine ended, he could have moved his family back to Canaan. However, he chose to stay in Egypt. This was his home, and he was committed to the work he had started. He remained loyal to Pharaoh because he recognized and appreciated what Pharaoh had done for him.

I am not suggesting we never pursue better opportunities. However, while we are where we are, be loyal to God, your relationships, and your current circle of influences. If God has devised a better opportunity for you, then pursue it. Generally, those you have served loyally will wish you the best and thank you for your loyalty.

I must be brutally honest and transparent. I have been guilty of disloyalty myself. A few years ago, I was working for a good company when a better opportunity came along with another company. It was a real struggle for me to decide what to do. In the end, I made the move, and it turned out to be a good move. However, I still feel badly for the people at that company who trusted me and placed confidence in me, only to have me "jump ship" a short time later. I am a very loyal person at heart.

Throughout my career and personal life, others have shown great loyalty to me, and I am grateful for it.

Perhaps most importantly, God has always shown tremendous loyalty to me. He has never walked away from me, even though I have walked away from him. He has never turned his back on me, even though I have turned my back on him many times. He has never denied me, even though I have denied him, if not literally or verbally, through my actions or inactions. With each passing day, I try to be mindful of God's loyalty to me, and I am working at remaining loyal to him.

Never forget where your allegiances lie. God deserves and expects our upmost loyalty. Second, our family deserves and expects our loyalty. Everything else is secondary. This is not to say we ignore the needs of others, but we must be loyal in this order. This hierarchy of loyalty sort of reminds me of an airplane flight. After you board, the flight attendant goes through the routine of the safety directions. First, she points out the exit doors. She reminds us that we cannot smoke in the restroom, and if we do, an alarm will be activated. She reminds us that if we tamper with the smoke detector in the restroom, we will be sent to federal prison. She reminds us how to use our seat cushion as a flotation device, even though we barely cross water during the flight. Then, she explains how, should the cabin lose oxygen during flight, our masks will drop down. She always explains to secure the oxygen supply to you before attempting to help anyone else with their oxygen. The reasoning behind this is that we will only function at our optimal level if we have the proper oxygen supply. Then, we can assist others who may need our help. Secondly, we would likely assist our family members or the people sitting closest to us during the flight. Finally, once our oxygen supply is restored, and our family's oxygen supply is restored, we can then assist everyone else throughout the cabin. Our loyalty should be similar. First, be loyal to God. He will give us the strength, energy, and ability we need to serve others. Then, we are loyal to our family. We provide and uplift and support them in everything. Then, once we are loyal to God and our family, we can then serve others effectively.

I love "March Madness" and the NCAA Men's Basketball tournament. Every year we love to see the upstart "Cinderella" teams bust a bracket or to watch the historical powerhouses win another championship. One of the most intriguing stories in men's basketball over the last few years has been that of Butler University in Indianapolis, Indiana.

Brad Stevens was a twenty-three-year-old pharmaceutical sales rep with a great future and great income potential, and he worked for one of the most respected pharmaceutical companies in the country. However, something deep down kept telling him he wanted to be a basketball coach. In 2000, he told his girlfriend of his dreams, and she advised him to take a chance and pursue coaching. So, Brad left the security and the comforts of a great job to pursue his goal. He first accepted a volunteer position at Butler University and quickly moved into a low-paying administrative position under head coach Thad Matta. Matta left Butler in 2001, and Stevens moved into a full-time assistant coach's position. Under new head coach Todd Lickliter, Stevens became more involved in the everyday aspects of the Butler program. In 2007, Lickliter left Butler and accepted another coaching position. Brad Stevens' dream of coaching an NCAA basketball team had come to pass. At 30 years old, Brad became one of the youngest head coaches in Division 1 basketball.

In 2010, Brad Stevens led the Butler Bulldogs on an historic run through the tournament field and landed in the national championship game against powerhouse Duke. The game was a thriller and came down to the last few seconds. Butler missed a heart-wrenching three point shot at the buzzer that would have given Butler the win. In the end, Duke won the game.

Usually, success like this leads to bigger, better, more lucrative coaching opportunities at high profile programs. Frankly, several schools courted Brad Stevens, and realistically, Butler probably could not pay him what some of these schools could have paid him. However, he decided to stay at Butler. He did receive an attractive raise and a contract extension, as he deserved, but he decided to stay with the school that gave him a chance and took a chance on him. In 2011, he led Butler to the national championship game again, this time losing to perennial powerhouse Connecticut. However, Butler continues to be a threat each year in the tournament, and Brad Stevens has remained loyal to Butler. When asked by a reporter if he would ever leave Butler, Stevens responded, "I guess, if they kicked me out." He also stated, "I am loyal to Butler." We all need to evaluate better opportunities, but we also need to be loyal to those who give us opportunities and chances. Joseph spent the remainder of his life working for Pharaoh. Pharaoh gave him his chance, and Joseph was loyal. Be loyal to God, be loyal to your family, and then be loyal to everyone else. Your life will then be a success.

Ironically, just as I was finishing this book, it was announced that Brad Stevens was leaving Butler University to accept the head coaching job with the Boston Celtics. This does not change my opinion regarding Brad's loyalty. He could have left the job for the first offer, but he stayed and helped establish the program into a perennial powerhouse before moving on to a great opportunity. These opportunities will arise in life, and we must seize them if they are right for us.

The Ending

In the end, Joseph was reunited with his family. At last, he had his brothers, his father, his wife, and his children surrounding him. Ultimately, his faithfulness and obedience was rewarded beyond measure. He saw the plan God had for his life unfold. He saw his destiny fulfilled, and experienced absolute success. I think if we truly give our all for God, we can experience this level of restoration and fulfillment in our lives. If we practice these attributes, we can be assured of a sense of completeness, fulfillment, and peace. I am sure that Joseph often questioned the course of his life, and pondered whether his dreams would come to pass. However, as mentioned many time before, he kept on keeping on.

Joseph's Success Saves the Region

If Joseph had not been obedient to his father and to God, if he had not been betrayed by his brothers, if he had not been sold to slave traders, accused of a horrible crime, and sent to prison, it is possible that the entire region would have suffered catastrophic consequences from the famine. However, because Joseph was faithful and because he practiced these attributes, the entire region of Egypt and Canaan was saved. Additionally, Joseph set in motion the events that would eventually lead to the exodus of the Hebrew nation out of Egypt almost three hundred years later. No one but Joseph could see the calamity that was coming. Not Pharaoh, not his dream readers, no one. Because of his faithfulness and trust in God, Joseph was exactly where he was supposed to be.

Success is Never Final

In my observations of successful people, I have also noticed this. Truly successful people are always looking for that next challenge. Even when they achieve their goals or obtain their objectives, they always see another challenge to confront or another opportunity to seize. That is how successful people are wired. Certainly, when we achieve success, we should pause and reflect, relish the victory, and savor the juices of the accomplishment. But truly successful people look ahead to another goal. They never become static. They constantly look for, and recognize, opportunities.

I am certain that Joseph accomplished much more after the famine. The author of Genesis fast forwards to the end of Joseph's life, but I am sure so much more happened in his later years. Keep the gears churning and keep the ideas flowing. Be observant and be alert for the next opportunity. God wants to challenge us and reward us with that great sense of success until the very end.

Complacency

As discussed earlier, never become complacent. Always be diligent. If you look at the many successful people who have experienced failure, you will notice that the failure often occurs at the pinnacle of their careers. A young, ambitious politician spends decades achieving the respect and power that comes from public office, only to leave it in disgrace because of scandal. A corporate CEO who has spent years of hard work and sacrifice to reach the top falls from grace due to greed or corruption. An athlete who has worked tirelessly to achieve world-wide superstar status has a dark secret exposed. We could count endless examples of those who have reached enviable levels of success and then toppled from the summit in disgrace. I think one of the many reasons this happens is complacency. These people forget what it took to get them to where they are. They dismiss the fact that they are vulnerable. Ultimately, they let down their guard.

In early May of 1996, several climbing expeditions were in pursuit of the summit on Mount Everest. Standing at 29,028 feet,

Mount Everest is the tallest mountain on earth and has claimed the lives of nearly a fourth of the people who have tried to reach its summit. At this altitude, the same altitude that most passenger jets fly, a human being only gets one fourth of the oxygen they get at sea level. Decision making skills, basic motor skills, and logic and reasoning are marginal at best.

Two of those teams, one led by Doug Fisher of Seattle, the other team led by Rob Hall of New Zealand, were tracking for the summit on May 10. Due to many delays, one caused by a "bottleneck" of climbers at the famed "Hillary Step," many of the climbers did not reach the summit until well after the mandated turn-around time decreed by Hall and Fisher. By the time these climbers started down, and while some, including Scott Fisher, were still reaching the summit, conditions worsened as a severe storm besieged the mountain. As you may recall, Hall, Fisher, and several other climbers died high on the mountain that night. 1996 turned out to be the deadliest climbing season ever until 2006. Many climbing experts have speculated and pondered as to why the disaster occurred. Certainly the storm was unexpected and unpredictable. Some of the climbers may have been overcome by "hypoxia" or altitude sickness. Some may have suffered cerebral or pulmonary edema.

Others have suggested that complacency may have played a role in the disaster. These guides had experienced tremendous success in the past with little or no trouble. It is possible, along with many other factors, that they let down their guard. It is easy to do when things go well for a time. We can never throw caution to the wind. Always be diligent; always be on guard. Success is fragile. If we become complacent, we could find ourselves trapped in the storm.

Never Forget Your Heritage

My dad was one of seven siblings born into a poor family in a small town in East Tennessee in the latter years of the Great Depression. His dad worked for a stove foundry in Cleveland, Tennessee, and he worked hard to provide for his large family. There were no excesses and no luxuries. My grandfather was able to provide the basic essentials to survive and grow up during one of the most challenging economic times in our country's history. While most Americans were poor by today's standards at that time, the poorest of the poor lived in East Cleveland. This was where my dad grew up.

While Dad was blessed and was able to move us into a nicer area of town later in life, he never really forgot those he grew up with. Some of the friends he grew up with were white, and some were black. It did not matter. He truly treated everyone the same. I remember in his later years, a lot of those acquaintances would stop by Dad's business and chat with him. It did not matter how busy he was. He always made time to stop and visit with them. Often, I figured they were there to borrow money that they would likely never pay back. I am sure Dad knew they would never pay him back as well, but he would always help them out. I think he felt that since he had been blessed, it was his duty to help these folks out when he could.

A few days after my dad's funeral in 1999, I picked up the visitor registry the funeral home had given the family. I flipped over to the first page and was surprised to see the first person that had signed the registry that afternoon was a friend of Dad's named John Lindsey. I had gotten to the funeral home early that afternoon and had never seen him there. He must have slipped in very early, paid his respects, and left as quietly as he came in.

John was a poor, uneducated, African-American with whom Dad had grown up with in East Cleveland. John had a large family, had suffered his share of challenges in life, and mainly worked minimum wage jobs and waded through poverty-like conditions his entire life. John was one of those friends Dad never forgot. While Dad had experienced success and moved up the ladder in life, he always made time to visit with John. I remember one Sunday afternoon Dad and I rode over to John's house to visit him and one of his sons, who was a paraplegic. Frankly, I was a little uncomfortable, but Dad was not.

As I looked at John's poorly scribbled signature in the funeral registry book, tears welled up in my eyes. I knew Dad would have been honored to know John was the first in line to pay his respects. Honestly, that would have meant more to Dad than if the Governor of the state had came by to visit. It touched me to think that John cared enough for Dad and appreciated Dad enough to be the first in line that afternoon. He did not want anyone to see him, and he did not want to draw attention to himself. He came by before anyone was even there, but he wanted to let Dad know he appreciated him.

While we may experience success in life, it is crucial that we remember, honor, and respect our heritage. I am one of the lucky ones. I grew up in a great home with great parents who loved, provided, and sacrificed beyond compare to give my brother and me what we needed. Everyone is not so fortunate. However, no matter what our heritage or background is, we can all look back and think of family members and friends who have inspired and mentored us. We can never forget them. Likewise, we must be aware that there is a generation behind us who needs the same support, sacrifice, and mentoring so they can achieve success in their lives. We need to make time to be there for those coming behind us. Joseph viewed his past with reverence, his present with reverence, and his future with reverence and respect.

Joseph did just that. Despite the betrayal by his brothers, and despite some of the dysfunctions of his family, he was honored and obligated to bring his family to Egypt to live out their lives. He would have not had it any other way. While Joseph integrated himself into Egyptian society, culture, and even married into an Egyptian family, he never forgot his Hebrew background. As a matter of fact, as I mentioned earlier, Joseph gave very specific instructions to have his bones returned to the land of his father's when they returned to Canaan. This proves two things, Joseph was keenly aware of and greatly appreciative of his family heritage, but he was also very aware of his spiritual heritage. He knew that the Hebrews would one day make an Exodus from Egypt, and he was preparing himself and his family for that fulfillment of prophecy.

Never think that your behaviors, actions, and decisions today will not impact the generations who come behind you. Jonathon Edwards was the young pastor who wrote and gave the famous "sinners in the hands of an angry God" sermon in 1800. Also, he was a key player in the first "great spiritual awakening" movement in our country. Some years after his death, some researchers conducted a study of the ancestors of Jonathon Edwards and the ancestors of another man who lived approximately the same time as Edwards and in the same community. This man, called "Max Jukes" (an alias), married a woman, and they went on to have many children. It was discovered that "Max Jukes," who presumably had no ties to any faith or religion, had approximately 540 descendants. Of these, 310 died as paupers, 150 were criminals with arrests for various crimes, 7 were convicted murderers, 100 were drunkards, addicts, and derelicts, and more than half the women who descended from this family turned out to be prostitutes, addicts, and wound up completely broke and indigent.

Jonathon Edwards married as well and went on to have eleven children, three sons, and eight daughters. Research was done on approximately 1,394 of his descendants. Through this research, it was discovered that 13 of Edward's descendants would turn out to be college presidents, 65 would become college professors, 3 would become United States senators, 30 would become judges, 100 would become lawyers, 60 would become physicians, 75 would become army and navy officers, 100 would become preachers and missionaries, 60 would become authors of prominence, and Edwards' grandson, Aaron Burr, would become Vice President of the United States, serving under Thomas Jefferson from 1801-1805.

There has been some dispute over the years about how the data and research on "Max Jukes" was collected and whether it is completely accurate. Even if the data on Jukes is incorrect or skewed, the pedigree and record of the descendants of Jonathan Edwards is absolutely true and well documented through American history and his family records. Edwards laid the foundation for the success of his family by understanding the importance of legacy and example. He recognized the importance of leading by example, and he understood how important it was to set a challenging precedent for his descendants to follow. He recognized the value of education and how it could empower and equip people for success and more fulfilling lives.

Epilogue

As the account of Joseph draws to an end, we learn that his family has moved to Egypt. Joseph's father, Jacob, blessed Joseph's two sons, and Joseph enjoyed his last few years with the peace of knowing he had fulfilled his purpose. He likely spent his last years and days reflecting on the amazing journey God had led him through. Surely he dwelled on those obstacles and opportunities God placed before him. As he neared the end, he observed the lives he had touched by adhering to these attributes.

One day, just like Joseph, we will near the end of our journey. I do not know what season of life you are in. You could be a young teenager in high school, a college student, a working professional, or a retired person. Whether you have fifty years left on your journey, or one week, it is never too late to examine our lives and seek to improve our existence.

Because of his obedience, commitment, and resilience, Joseph was fortunate to end his journey knowing he had experienced true success, fulfillment, and purpose. I can only hope when my destination is in sight, and my journey is nearing its end, that I can say I experienced at least a glimpse of this type of success, fulfillment, and purpose. I can only imagine that this type of joy will make the transition to eternity much more rewarding.

Genesis ends with Joseph's death and burial. Exodus begins roughly two hundred and seventy-five years later. Unfortunately, the author or authors of Genesis and Exodus skipped the vast period in between. I would have been curious to see what kind of lives Joseph's children lived; what kind of success and impact they experienced. However, without knowing, I suspect Manasseh and Ephraim lived very successful lives. Joseph and his wife laid the foundation for their offspring to succeed, and Joseph and his wife left a legacy for them to follow, be proud of, and to continue.

While we do not like to think about or dwell on our eventual demise, I encourage you to think about your epitaph, or think about what others will say about you when you are gone. What would you want your family and friends to say about you when they celebrate your life? I hope mine will read something like this:

- He glorified God!
- He was a great husband!
- He was a great father who loved to laugh with his family!
- He was a caring and giving friend, son, brother, and co-worker!
- He encouraged others!
- He made a difference in the lives of others!
- He was a success!
- He left this world in better shape than he found it!

I truly hope you will be inspired, motivated, and re-invigorated from this book. More than anything, I want you, and me, to experience success, fulfillment, and purpose in life as Joseph experienced. Do not underestimate yourself. God has great things in store for us if we can adhere to the attributes.

As I have mentioned several times, integrating these attributes into our life does not insure that we will not have hardships and setbacks. It does not guaranty that we will amass a fortune or material wealth. It does not imply we are meant to be the CEO of a Fortune 500 company. It does imply that if we do these things that Joseph did, we can experience a sense of success, fulfillment, and purpose in our lives that so many are deprived of. Sensing success, fulfillment, and purpose comes from living a meaningful life wherever you may be and whatever role you may be. The sense of success, fulfillment, and purpose comes from knowing we gave our best, did what was right, and sought God's wisdom and divine intervention in our lives; that we did things honestly and the best we could; we had our motives in the right place.

Most of us will likely never be second in command of a great nation. However, we can make a substantial impact and contribution in the lives of those we love, touch, work for, and those around the world that desperately need help. Most importantly, we can live out our full potential, the potential that God bestowed upon us, if we will only seek his counsel, wisdom, and serve him with the purest and sincerest of intentions.

Finally, as I have said several times in this book, I am not suggesting you should try to change your personality. Each one of us is a unique, special creation with unmatched skills and abilities. If you are an extravert, be an extravert. If you are introvert, be an introvert. If you are analytical, be analytical. If you are a right-brain thinker, be a right-brain thinker. Always be yourself, and be proud of yourself. Working these attributes into your life does not mean you change who you are; you just change how you view things, accomplish things, and maybe how you view your interaction with others. Always be transparent. I had a boss once that always reminded me that it takes most people about two minutes to "size you up" and determine what kind of person you are. You may be able to fool some people for a short time. But you will not fool people for long.

Success is a fluid endeavor. You never reach the peak. You never accomplish everything you hope and long to accomplish. True success is never final. Each accomplishment is just one more accomplishment. Relish, ponder, and treasure each success. Then, after a time, seek the next challenge. Resolve to seize the challenge and emerge triumphant again. Seek God's guidance, wisdom, and intuition. Then, patiently await the thunder of his response.

I hope this book will challenge you to overcome self-imposed limitations. Joseph is living proof that God does guide our lives, even when it appears to be out of control. God can make great things happen out of our seemingly desperate circumstances. Accept and thank God for where you are today. Joseph's life is an affirmation of faithfulness being rewarded. Trust and believe that God has the best in store for you.

Assess and understand your strengths and your gifts. Make sure you are utilizing your gifts in the most effective way. Think about where you want to be in the next five to ten years. Does this plan include God? Dwell on the impact you want to leave for your family and for mankind. Embrace each moment with a sense of urgency.

As a great philosopher once said, "For a ship with no port in mind there is no favorable wind." You have to know where you want to go. Seek clarity about the direction in your life. Talk to God and make sure it is where he wants you to go. If you both agree, nothing will stop you from achieving your goals. Approach life with a grateful heart and be thankful for the loved ones in your life. Never take one day for granted. Tell the ones you love you love them every day.

Bibliography

Aboutpittsburgh.com (2006) Albrecht Powell-Sago mining accident.

Collateral (2004). Movie, Paramount Pictures/DreamWorks SKG, screenplay by Stuart Beattie.

Holy Bible, New International Version® (1973, 1978, 1984). International Bible Society, Zondervan Publishing House.

John Gottman (2012). Article on relationships, The Gottman Institute, University of Seattle.

Kelly McDonald (2012). Presentation at Tennessee Bankers Association. "Changing demographics and the impact on your business."

Success Magazine (2011). Quotes from Rob Lowe.

Time Magazine (1991). Article on Lee Atwater, February 1991 edition.

Yahoo Sports (2011) Paula Thompson. Bobby Allison NASCAR Hall of fame.

CPSIA information can be obtained at www.ICGtesting.com
Printed in the USA
LVOW12s0212101213

364568LV00001B/81/P